LIBRARY - Islington Sixth Form Centre

D1426352

CITY & ISLINGTON COLLEGE

SB001164

The Black Tradition in American Dance

The Black Tradition in American Dance

Richard A. Long

Photographs selected and annotated by

Joe Nash

PRION

Dedicated to Katherine Dunham and Pearl Primus

Acknowledgements

I am deeply indebted to Joe Nash for his assistance and contribution to this project. The various stages of the manuscript were all "processed" by Carolyn Clark, who also contributed research assistance. My research assistant Rebecca Sharpless has been most helpful. The American Dance Festival project "The Black Tradition in American Modern Dance," directed by Gerald Myers and Stephanie Rinehart, provided several useful encounters with Bill Moore, Zita Allen, Brenda Dixon-Stovell and Joe Nash. Over the years I have gathered insight and information from association with Marion Cuyjet, Katherine Dunham, Pearl Primus, Rex Nettleford, Alvin Ailey, Maya Angelou, Carmencita Romero, Romare Bearden, Nanette Bearden, Lavinia Williams, Louis Johnson, and Helen Armstead Johnson.

I am indebted to dozens and dozens of people who answered inquiries or who supplied materials. An attempt to provide a complete list of such persons would flirt with disaster and so I simply say a heartfelt thank you.

R.A.L.

Islington
Sixth Form
Centre

LIBRARY
793.3
03956

First published in the United Kingdom by
PRION
an imprint of Multimedia Books Limited,
32–34 Gordon House Road, London NW5 1LP

Text copyright © Richard A. Long 1989
Compilation copyright © Multimedia Books Limited 1989

Editor: Susan Rea
Design: Behram Kapadia
Production: Hugh Allan

All rights reserved. No part of this publication may be reproduced or transmitted in any form or by any means, electronic or mechanical, including photocopying or recording, or by any information storage and retrieval system, without permission in writing from the publisher and copyright holders.

British Library Cataloguing in Publication Data
Long, Richard A. 1927–
    The black tradition in American dance Richard A. Long
    1. United States. Dancing to 1979
    I. Title
    793.3'0973

ISBN 1–85375–046–8

Typesetting by Wyvern Typesetting Limited, Bristol, UK
Origination by J. Films, Bangkok, Thailand
Printed in Hong Kong by Imago Publishing

Contents

1 *The Tradition Emerges*

John Parks and Sara Yarborough in a 1973 performance of Alvin Ailey's 1958 Blues Suite.

Poster: Dance Black America, Brooklyn Academy of Music, 1983.

*A*ll dance conceived and performed by human beings is human dance. "Human," however, is rather an abstract concept; people are more generally perceived as belonging to groupings such as races, nations, classes, believers, and an infinite array of other categories. In the United States the most fundamental social reality has been the distinction between white and non-white, and a range of usually invidious social practices based upon the distinction has served to isolate and detract from the Black minority – particularly Afro-Americans – culturally, economically, and politically.

This social reality emerges in every area, including dance, in which discussion of the Afro-American presence and experience is conducted. The term "Black dance", for instance, though widely used, poses questions and problems which can, perhaps, never be resolved to general satisfaction. The critics Zita Allen and Brenda Dixon-Stowell each wrote on aspects of this topic in *The Black Tradition in American Modern Dance* (1988). Stowell says, for example, "I do not believe that Alvin Ailey and Arthur Mitchell conceive their choreography as Black dance. Black influences are one of the many influences in their works." And she cautions later, "Any serious attempt to study Black dance demands a study of African and New World Black cultures." Zita Allen is more peremptory: "Does 'Black Dance' really exist? And if in fact it does, just who is qualified to define it?" She arrives at the conclusion:

> I think it is presumptuous for any one person – black or white – to presume to define "Black Dance." Since its existence was declared, far too many critics have taken the term and its murky definitions for granted.

In the same collection, however, dance critics William Moore, Joe Nash, and Richard A. Long, all of an older generation than Dixon-Stowell and Allen, do take the term for granted, however warily.

The mere physical presence of Black dancers in a modern dance work or in a classical ballet clearly should not invoke the use of the term "Black dance"; however, the social or cultural setting obtrudes upon our perception, sometimes with surprising and even deplorable consequences. Such consequences, being the product of the social milieu, will only change as that does.

Clearly dance that arises in a culture or a cultural milieu which – for whatever reason – is called Black, may be called Black dance (in the same way in which music so circumstanced is called Black music). Such cultures include those of sub-Saharan Africa, and the Africanized components of Western-hemisphere cultures such as the Afro-American, the Afro-Brazilian, the Afro-Cuban. In other words, Black dance, Black stance and Black gesture are non-verbal patterns of body gestures and expressions which are distinctively Black African or originate from their descendents elsewhere.

Contemporary American concert-theatrical dance exists in a culturally diverse milieu, so that the term "Black dance" in this domain reflects a social as much as a cultural distinction. In this book we will trace the Black tradition as it has given rise to current Afro-American dance trends and achievements, looking at Black presence and influence in various categories of dance. These include the direct inclusion of Black choreographic movement in a theatrical work, as in the Haitian-derived works of Katherine Dunham, or of popular dance-hall forms in works of Talley Beatty; the absorption of Black choreographic talent in a choreographed role, particularly in musical theater, such as that of Katherine Dunham in *Cabin in the Sky* on Broadway; the mimetic reflection of Black choreographic movement in work by a variety of choreographers, particularly those of Broadway shows; the absorption of Black stance and gesture into a choreographic matrix, as in the work of Jerome Robbins and Twyla Tharpe; and the choreographic interpretation of Black music and musical elements, such as spirituals, blues, jazz, samba, or their distinctive features, as in the work of Helen Tamiris and many others.

What About the Music?

Dance is normally performed to musical accompaniment which may range from simple hand-clapping to elaborate choral and orchestral structures, as well as today's synthesized sound structures. Throughout the history of American concert-theatrical dance, Black music has been drawn upon by both Black and white choreographers and dancers as an accompanying medium. Black music may be defined as that music whose origins lie clearly in the social setting of Black culture, either in Africa or in the diaspora. In the United States the term is most commonly understood to apply to that music which springs from the sphere of Afro-American culture, comprehending three large chronologically overlapping segments: folk-rural, folk-urban, and trans-urban. From the folk-rural culture came the spirituals and work songs. The blues straddle the folk-rural and the folk-urban, while from the latter grew ragtime and early jazz. The trans-urban culture saw the further development of jazz into swing, bebop, and fusion, as well as the growth of gospel music.

Peripheral to Black music proper have been the lively and sentimental minstrel songs written by composers such as Stephen Foster (who was white) and James Bland (who was Black), and the adaptations, arrangements, settings, and metamorphoses of Black music elements in the work of other American composers ranging from Louis Gottschalk to George Gershwin, William Grant Still, Leonard Bernstein and Harold Arlen. Black musical elements, too, though frequently in an unidiomatic fashion, have been used by European composers. These include Dvořák, Debussy, Ravel, Milhaud and Stravinsky.

Individual dancers and choreographers who want to make use of Black music and its peripheral genres have a number of possibilities open to them: they can use a dance vocabulary derived largely from Black dance, stance and gesture, or they can use a vocabulary drawn from another tradition (such as ballet or a specific "modern" school), but adopt its phrasing and accents to the music; or they can devise a vocabulary in a decorative or incidental manner so that the movement in large part is counterpoised to the music, or has no direct reference to it. (The first two instances can properly be referred to as examples of the Black presence in dance, while the status of the last is ambiguous.)

One of the leading theorists of the American modern dance was Louis Horst, who was associated as music director with many of its pioneers; he taught dance composition to hundreds of aspirant choreographers. In his assembled notes published as *Modern Dance Forms*, he offered the following reflections on jazz:

> Although jazz is by now cosmopolitan and international, and has proved its affinity to the whole modern world by its popularity with all races and cultures, still it is most typically American. It is natural to all Americans, as deeply and subconsciously understood as any other folk dance is understood by people from whom it grew. It is specifically the expression of present-day urban America. It is an intimate part of our daily life and shows in the urban walk, the posture, the rhythm of speech, the gesture, the costumes, of the city.

In a sense, Horst was using jazz as a metaphor for Afro-American music generally.

Looking Back

In the nineteenth century Black dance, stance, and gesture were a staple of popular entertainment in the United States, albeit in a grossly caricatured form.

White Minstrels

White performers in blackface gamboled, cavorted, and stumbled on stage for the benefit of other whites who drew vast amusement from the perceived idiosyncracies of Black movement styles. One of the most popular stage acts of the 1830s was the "Jim Crow" routine of Thomas D. Rice, a blackface performance, which included a song and a dance said to be based on one he had actually seen performed by a crippled elderly Black.

Thomas Rice became famous for his "Jim Crow" routine.

JIM CROW.
NEW YORK.

Isolated imitations of Blacks in popular variety shows gradually gave rise to the blackface minstrel show, a paradoxical and ironical genre. Arriving at a distinctive format in the 1840s in the North, it consisted in its developed form of three parts. The opening found the performers, all in blackface, sitting in a semicircle, an interlocutor or master-of-ceremonies in the center, and the endmen, Mr. Tambo and Mr. Bones, seated at either end. The talents of each performer were displayed in this opening section, which consisted chiefly of song and comic dialect. The second part, called the olio, presented specialty acts, including a mock-oration known as a stump speech. It was usually in the olio that the most energetic Negro or "coon" dancing was offered up for the delectation of the audience. The third section of the standard minstrel show presented a dramatized musical sketch of "plantation" life that might be sentimental or burlesque, and which usually included more dancing.

The white dance performers in blackface minstrel shows in the 1840s and later undoubtedly incorporated actual elements of Black dance, stance and gesture in their performances, for there is abundant evidence that they observed Black recreational activity, which included dancing, particularly in border states such as Ohio.

Master Juba
At least one Black dancer, William Henry Lane, became famous as an occasional performer in white minstrel shows. Known as Master Juba, it is significant that he was regarded as the best dancer in the minstrel style.

"The Old Plantation" by an unknown artist in the 1790s shows a "stick dance" somewhere in South Carolina.

10

William Henry Lane, known as "Juba," learned clog-dancing at Irish socials in New York's Five Points district.

Lane represents an independent Black dance tradition, since he is said to have learned his craft from an older Black dancer known as Uncle Jim Lowe. In New York City, in the 1840s, Lane and other Black dancers performed in "low-life" settings before audiences of Blacks and Irishmen. A cultural interchange took place between Blacks and Irishmen at this point, accounting for the incorporation of the Irish jig and clog-dancing in a Black tradition which eventually produced tap-dancing. Lane was known as a jig-dancer.

Charles Dickens reports on the performance of a Black dancer in his *American Notes* and, while he does not mention Lane by name in the report, the description is of a breathtaking and unique performance. It is significant that Lane went to England in 1848 as a member of a group known as Pell's Ethiopian Serenaders. He died there in 1852, while probably still in his mid-twenties. In her article "Juba and American Minstrelsy", in *Chronicles of the American Dance*, Hannah Winter says of Lane, "This most influential single performer of nineteenth-century American dance was a prodigy of our entire theatrical history."

One of the English critics quoted by Winter observed:

... the dancing of Juba exceeded anything ever witnessed in Europe. The style as well as the execution is unlike anything ever seen in this country. The manner in which he beats time with his feet, and the extraordinary command he possesses over them can only be believed by those who have been present at his exhibition.

Of his impact in minstrelsy, Winter asserts that because of his influence "the minstrel-show dance retained more integrity as a Negro art form than any other theatrical derivative of Negro culture."

Black Minstrels

There had been some short-lived minstrel troupes made up of Black performers in the 1850s, the decade before the Civil War. Immediately after the War, however, Black minstrelsy emerged as a distinct stream. While Blacks at first took a leading role in forming and managing their own troupes, white entertainment professionals eventually dominated the field. The most exceptional Black manager was Charles Hicks, himself a performer, who found his greatest success in touring his companies abroad, particularly in Australia.

Dancing in the Black minstrel tradition was undoubtedly more diversified than it had been in the white companies, but it was still part of a variety show and did not attain a truly independent character, consisting chiefly in the performance of isolated turns and numbers. It is certain, however, that the third act "walk-around" in the Black minstrel tradition was more elaborate and dignified than in the white minstrel shows, usually taking the form of the cakewalk.

The Birth of Musical Comedy

Shortly after the appearance of considerable numbers of Black minstrel troupes on the traveling circuits, a trend away from blackface cavorting began in white minstrel shows (though it never disappeared entirely, and blackface appearances by whites remained a staple of American comedy entertainment, in stage and film productions, until the 1930s). The trend toward the exotic and the elegant in white minstrel shows may have been, in part, reaction to and even imitation of Black minstrelsy, but the

Christy's Minstrels, New York City, about 1844.

greatest influence was probably an immensely successful musical production. Ironically, it was called *The Black Crook*. A group of dancers had
been imported from Europe to appear in a production at New York's
Academy of Music. A fire at this building effectively canceled those plans,
whereupon the proprietor of a popular theater, Niblo's Garden, decided
to incorporate them, their costumes and special effects, into a pan-
tomime-style production for his theater. At much expense, and featuring
what was designated as the "Grand Parisienne Ballet Troupe," the
production opened in September 1866, to great acclaim. *The Black Crook*
ran for over a year, a truly remarkable run for the period, and was
followed at Niblo's Garden with a copycat production, *The White Faun*.

Whereas minstrelsy, white and Black, was presented exclusively by
males to overwhelmingly male audiences, the Niblo Garden show
featured the presence of women on the stage, and attracted more refined
audiences, consisting of both sexes. These shows, therefore, announced

the birth of musical comedy, and while the new genre existed for a long time parallel to minstrelsy, it was in the ascendant.

Early Black Musical Theater
In his historical record, *American Musical Theatre: A Chronicle*, Gerald Bordman roughly divides and classifies the earlier period before the birth of the truly modern musical as follows:

1866–78   Opera-bouffe, with native elements
1878–92   Impact of Gilbert and Sullivan
1892–1902 Further British influence and new stirrings
1902–7   Emergence of American talent
1907–14   Viennese influence

The Black musical theater flickered without actually flourishing, on a separate and unequal basis, in the third and fourth of these periods. The Black musical derived from Black minstrelsy, a tradition which itself continued to survive in obscure and far-flung areas of the Black belt until well into the first decades of the twentieth century, though it should be pointed out that some of Black minstrelsy was absorbed into vaudeville or variety entertainment by the end of the nineteenth century.

The manner in which the Black musicals came into being has made a fully documented presentation of their origins and character difficult, for they were usually organized on the road and often never came to New York at all. Speaking of the first of these shows, Edith Isaacs, in *The Negro in the American Theatre*, says:

> A change may be said to have begun when Sam Jack, a manager of a burlesque circuit, decided to arrange a complete show with Negro performers. *The Creole Show* was planned on the general pattern of the minstrels with one major innovation. It featured a chorus of sixteen beautiful Negro girls who sang and danced. The show opened in Boston in 1891, went on to Chicago and played at Sam

Buck-dancing contests closed the first part of this touring show (1897–1920).

13

Jack's Opera House there during the entire season of the World's Fair [1893]. For five years, in one form or another, *The Creole Show* went on.

Subsequent research has been unable to verify all of the facts; nevertheless, there is general agreement that *The Creole Show* marked a turning point and pointed the direction for a new genre. Many imitations followed. A definite dance finale, either the cakewalk or walkaround, usually characterized these shows. According to Katherine Dunham, in her essay "The Negro Dance,"

> The cakewalk tradition may properly be considered the urbanization of the plantation folk-dances, incorporating in the whole such separate figures as the Black Annie, the Pas Mala, the Strut, the Palmer House, and later Walkin' the Dog, Ballin' the Jack, and other individual expressions.

However, there is no doubt that the term cakewalk was applied to a wide range of choreographic inventions in which solo and couple elegance and virtuosity varied with the skill of the performers.

The year 1898 was a significant year for the Black musical, for it saw the production of two major pieces, both of which enter the New York annals: *A Trip to Coontown* (which did not have the cakewalk finale) and *Clorindy, Or the Origin of the Cake Walk*. *A Trip to Coontown* found its title and basic idea in the continuing Broadway fascination with the exotic: the prototype of the show, *A Trip to Chinatown*, had been the greatest hit of the 1890s.

A Trip to Coontown, Bordman says, played briefly at an "off-Broadway" theater, but

> ... was a landmark in that it was entirely written, performed, and produced by blacks. It was the creation of two particularly talented Negroes, Bob Cole and Billy Johnson .... The show created no stir on Broadway, but New Yorkers would shortly pay more respectful attention to Cole and the two Johnson brothers (Rosamond and J.W.) with whom he worked.

Clorindy, Or the Origin of the Cake Walk was essentially a music and dance afterpiece with music by Will Marion Cook and a libretto by Paul Laurence Dunbar. It had a large cast and its star was the dancer-comedian Ernest Hogan.

Another landmark in Black musical theater was the production in 1903 of *In Dahomey* with music by Will Marion Cook, lyrics by Paul Laurence Dunbar, and a libretto by J. A. Shipp. The production was definitely a star vehicle since it featured the team of Williams and Walker, comedians who used song and dance in their characterizations, though Walker was the more distinctive dancer. *In Dahomey* contained the now-expected cakewalk finale, with the audience participating by selecting the winner with its applause. After a New York run of less than two months, though that was considered phenomenal for a Black musical, the show went to London — where it ran for seven months.

Williams and Walker repeated the pattern with the much less successful *In Abyssinia* (1904) and the more successful *Bandana Land* (1908), in which the dancing was reputedly spectacular. The partnership of Williams and Walker was broken following this show, due to Walker's

Holidays, Saturday nights, special events, or just the need for amusement at the Big House, were occasions for singing and dancing on plantations.

The Walkers, Ada and George, delighted American and European audiences with their cakewalk in the Williams and Walker operetta In Dahomey.

Williams and Walker made the cakewalk an international favorite.

Eddie Rector "traveled across the stage with superb grace and elegance," and influenced many class act teams.

illness. In 1910 Williams went into the *Ziegfeld Follies*, which had begun in 1907.

At this time the Black musical disappeared from Broadway; however the development of the Harlem community provided hospitality for a show which had begun in 1911 in Washington, D.C. *Dark Town Follies* opened in 1913 at the Lafayette Theatre in Harlem. This show went through a long run, later moving downtown to be seen by white audiences. Its two tap-dancing stars, who were to have long careers, were Toots Davis and Eddie Rector. The female dancing star was Ethel Williams, who was delegated to teach the show's finale to the cast of the *Ziegfeld Follies* of 1914 after Ziegfeld bought the number for his show. Of this transposition Carl Van Vechten observes:

> . . . the effect was not the same. The tunes remained pretty; the *Follies* girls undoubtedly were pretty, but the rhythm was gone, the thrill was lacking, the boom was inaudible, the Congo had disappeared.

Concert-Theatrical Dance

There is a gradation of prestige among the types of dance performance available to today's public. Occupying the first rank, and comparable to other "serious" genres such as opera and legitimate theater, is the variety of dance, in ballet, modern and other idioms, which we designate concert-theatrical dance, offered by such companies as the New York City Ballet, the Martha Graham Dance Company, the Alvin Ailey American Dance Theater and various national folk dance companies. Ranking slightly below these, and drawing on both dancers and choreographers trained in the same schools and traditions, is the show dancing of Broadway and regional theater. The chief difference between concert-theatrical dance and show dancing is a functional one. For the former the dance work, composition, piece, or "ballet" (there is no agreed upon and satisfactory name for the choreographed piece) is autonomous (self-contained), while in the latter it is linked to a larger work in any number of possible ways. Somewhat below show dancing in prestige is the episodic choreography of backup dancers in pop and rock music spectaculars, and the choreographic episodes of music videos.

Show dancing and the dancing of backup groups may be regarded as the descendants of dancing in early musical shows and in vaudeville; dancing in music videos owes something, but not everything, to film dancing as it developed in the 1920s and 1930s. Modern American concert-theatrical dancing derives from a number of early twentieth-century precursors, but an irreducible list would mention at least three, Isadora Duncan, Sergey Diaghilev, and Denishawn.

Isadora Duncan

The name of Isadora Duncan summons up the idea of freeing the body and the soul of the dancer from systems and allowing it to express more freely the inspiration which comes from plastic art, music, and poetry. Her doctrine influenced generations of hazily "interpretive" dancers in the United States. Her great personal impact, however, clearly derived from a more definite realization in her practice of a powerful concept of

Florence Mills.

Christian Holder in Trinity, Joffrey Ballet Company, 1970.

dance and choreography. An early observer, Carl Van Vechten, then a *New York Times* music critic, noted in 1909:

> Miss Isadora Duncan, who has evolved a style of choreographic art which corresponds in a measure at least . . . with the dances of the ancient Greeks, made her reappearance in New York last·evening at the Metropolitan Opera House . . .

Isadora Duncan, who indeed made constant allusions to ancient Greece in both her words and movement, had left the United States to go to Europe where, as early as 1900, she presented her dances in Paris as the embodiment of a new aesthetic. In succeeding years she performed, proselytized, took students, and established schools. She became better known than any other dancer in the world, and an inspiration to a variety of artists. Her travels included Russia where in 1905 she met Diaghilev and Stanislavsky, both of whom were impressed by her.

Though Duncan pursued her career in Europe, Americans heard of her frequently. She was in the United States in 1915 and 1916, and again in 1922 when she performed in New York, Boston and Indianapolis. The fact that her death was noted at the same time as that of Florence Mills, in the December 1927 issue of *Crisis*, bespeaks the interest that some Afro-Americans took in her career and its accents of individual freedom.

Sergey Diaghilev

Sergey Diaghilev, neither a choreographer nor a dance theorist but an art critic and impresario, assembled a company of Russian dancers and took them to Paris and London in 1909, thus creating a new impulse in dance. Theatrical dance in the West at that time was moribund; Diaghilev introduced a new choreographic genre, the short ballet. Essentially the creation of Fokine, exemplified in such ballets as *Les Sylphides, Schéhérazade,* and *The Firebird,* the short ballet made possible a diverse experience in one evening, with sharply contrasting music, settings, and dance movement. The Diaghilev-Fokine innovation, unknown at the time in Russia itself and still not common there, was to become the staple of concert-theatrical dance in the West.

There are differing views concerning the extent to which Fokine may have been influenced by the less systematic Isadora Duncan; certainly parallels exist between his work and her statements and practice.

While the Russian dancers Anna Pavlova and Mikhail Mordkin appeared in the United States in 1910, and though there was an attempt to pirate the success of the Diaghilev company in 1911 by Gertrude Hoffman, who appeared with a "Russianized" troupe at the Winter Garden in New York, the Diaghilev company was first seen in New York at the Metropolitan Opera House in 1916. Initially they disappointed Carl Van Vechten, who had seen them in Paris, but the arrival of Nijinsky in April 1916 galvanized the company and electrified the New York public. The new ballet had come decisively to America.

Denishawn

In many ways, the quintessential American dancer of the early decades of the century was Ruth St. Denis. About the same age as Isadora Duncan, she came to the dance somewhat later, following a brief career as an actress. Her full commitment to dance began in 1906 with the solo piece

Radha, inspired by an illustration in a cigarette advertisement. After an early successful concert tour she went to Europe, following in the wake of other American female dancers such as Loie Fuller, Maud Allan, and, of course, Isadora Duncan. She had three successful years of touring there, but returned to the United States in 1909. Isadora Duncan (and Maud Allan) had looked to Greek Sculpture for inspiration, but Ruth St. Denis remained faithful to the living Orient which had first inspired her, ultimately drawing on China, Japan, and Java, as well as India and Siam for inspiration.

In 1914 she was joined by Ted Shawn who became her partner, husband, and collaborator, and out of their joint energies emerged the Denishawn School of Dancing and Related Arts, which was to mark profoundly the dance in America. Aggressive touring and the creation of a school of the dance with satellite operations spread the fame and influence of Denishawn far and wide, the greatest impact occurring in the 1920s. Though the predominant inspiration for St. Denis remained the Orient, Shawn, in his work, turned to Native American and to American folk material, including that of Black America. (The organization disbanded in 1931 after St. Denis and Shawn separated.)

Dance Theatre of Harlem in Paquita, *1980.*

Blacks in Concert-Theatrical Dance

American concert-theatrical dance assumed its definitive form in the six or eight years between the earliest performances of modern dance pioneers Martha Graham, Doris Humphrey and Charles Weidman, and Helen Tamiris (1926–8) and the creation of the American Ballet Company (1934) by George Balanchine and Lincoln Kirstein. During this period (which also saw significant dance activity by other figures such as Ruth Page, Agnes de Mille, Hanya Holm, Lester Horton, and Ted Shawn), Black pioneers, notably Hemsley Winfield, Edna Guy, Asadata Dafora, and Katherine Dunham, were also engaged in developing and creating dance language and dance works.

American social restrictions served to inhibit any profound interaction between whites and Blacks in this earlier period, though some limited interaction did, in fact, take place. In general, the modern dance was more hospitable to the idea of using Black dancers and Black material, in part because of its focus on the American scene and on social consciousness, in part because its audiences, concentrated in the Northeast, were more progressive and liberal. Ballet, on the other hand, was perceived by its audience to be Euro-classical and to be antipathetic to the presence of Blacks on stage.

Beyond the attitudes of the audiences, however, lay other considerations. Modern dance accepted and used a variety of body types. In ballet, the notion of ideal body types prevailed, types to which few Blacks conformed to the satisfaction of choreographers and public.

In the years before World War II, however, the question of Blacks in ballet was, in fact, almost entirely theoretical, since few Blacks had any prospect of overcoming the hurdle of being accepted for ballet training. In the years following World War II, as training opportunities for all kinds of dance expanded, Blacks began to be recruited into modern dance companies, though nothing comparable happened in ballet. By the late 1950s there was a profusion of Black activity in modern dance with the arrival on scene of Ailey, McKayle, Beatty, and others. Effective Black presence in ballet had to wait another decade until Arthur Mitchell, armed with the prestige of a career as soloist with the New York City Ballet, created the Dance Theatre of Harlem (DTH).

2 *Theater, Dance Hall, Concert Hall*

Florence Mills, Shuffle Along, *1921.*

Poster for the Cotton Club revue in Paris.

*T*he period from the end of the World War I to the beginning of the administration of Franklin D. Roosevelt (1918–32) can be divided into the Twenties proper (the so-called Roaring Twenties or Jazz Age) and the early Depression. The first part of this period coincides with the time when an essentially nationwide movement of artistic exploration and exhilaration occurred among Black Americans, with many major theatrical, musical, and literary events centered in New York City and in Harlem. This came to be known as the "Harlem Renaissance."

American life itself, despite the winning of a "War for Democracy," was rigidly segregated along color lines, even in New York City. It was a life which was to be strongly affected by progress and growth in three technological media; electrical sound recording, the expansion of film production and its transformation by sound recording, and the meteoric development of radio broadcasting.

For the chronicler of American musical theater, Gerald Bordman, the Broadway musicals of the period divide into those of the "Cinderella Era" of the early 1920s followed by those of the beginning of the "Golden Age of the American Musical." The separate Black musicals do not fit neatly into such a category, but their presence and impact was to affect the white musicals of the period, particularly in the area of show dancing, as was duly noted in the song sung by Golda Gray in the *Ziegfeld Follies* of 1922, "It's Getting Dark on Old Broadway."

A second influence on the dance of the period was the settling in the United States of a succession of major figures from the new ballet. Michel Fokine himself opened a school in New York in 1921 and contributed two dance sequences to the *Ziegfeld Follies* of 1922. Mikhail Mordkin, acclaimed as the virile partner of Pavlova years before, began his American career in 1923, appearing in the *Greenwich Village Follies* in 1924. A definitive new chapter in the history of the ballet in America was to open with the arrival of George Balanchine at the end of 1933.

The third influence on dance in the 1920s was the flourishing of Denishawn, and the onset of the new American dance derived in part from it. In a succession of tours, Denishawn offered elaborate spectacles ranging from "visualizations" of European concert music to a vast assortment of Oriental dance conceptions, and dances to the music of American composers. In 1925–6, Denishawn made a pilgrimage to the Far East, the source of much of its inspiration, appearing in Japan, China, Burma, India, Ceylon, and Java, among other places. Study with local dance teachers and observation led to an expansion of the Oriental repertory of the company. Successive defections from Denishawn during the 1920s by Louis Horst, the music director, and the dancers Martha Graham, Doris Humphrey, and Charles Weidman, were to be rich with consequence for dance in America. Martha Graham, who had appeared as a solo dancer in the *Greenwich Follies* of 1923, presented her first New York concert in the modern mode in 1926.

The first New York concert by Humphrey and Weidman was in 1928. The year before, the dancer Helen Tamiris, who had been a member of the Metropolitan Opera corps de ballet and a featured dancer in the *Music Box Revue*, had given a New York concert of "Dance Moods." The connecting link among all of these expressions of a new dance was Louis Horst, who was at the piano at all three events.

Christena Schlundt, in her chronicle of the career of Tamiris, reports on a failed initiative for the new dance:

> [Tamiris] proposed the Dance Repertory Theater . . . four of them would band together to give a series of their individual works each season at a common time and at a common theater with a single staff. . . . Martha Graham, Doris Humphrey, and Charles Weidman joined with her for two seasons, winters 1930 and 1931 (Agnes de Mille appeared during the second year) with Louis Horst as Musical Director.

Incompatibilities ended the Dance Repertory Theater after the second season, but the new dance flourished.

What Shall the Negro Dance About?

The Workers' Dance League, which came into being in the early 1930s to pursue a program of making the dance relevant to the masses, was an umbrella organization which included a diversity of subgroups. Opposed to art for art's sake, or dance for the sake of dance, it began in late 1933 a series of "forum recitals," the first of which was held October 1, at the Harlem YWCA. The topic was "What Shall the Negro Dance About?" probably a riposte to an article by Doris Humphrey, "What Shall We Dance About?" which had appeared in the quarterly *Trend* the year before. Prior to the discussion there was a performance by Hemsley Winfield and the ensemble of the New Negro Art Theater Dance Group of seven pieces from their repertory. The discussion was led by Winfield and the sculptor Augusta Savage, a leading pedagogic influence on the arts in Harlem at that time. Participants in the discussion included Add Bates, who said, "A Young Negro should dance about the things that are vital to

Hemsley Winfield's New Negro Art Theater Dance Group *in his* Life and Death. *(Winfield is on the floor.)*

Add Bates, 1933.

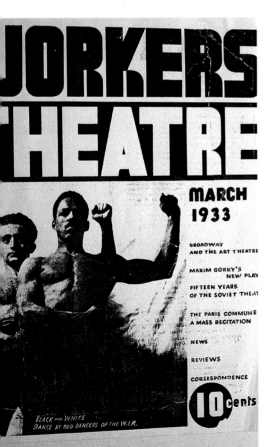

him." Bates was later to appear with Edith Segal and as the General in Weidman's *Candide*. A woman, not named in reports of the meeting, said, "We have come to a new type of dance, a dance that has social significance – our dance should express the strivings of the New Negro." It was not by chance that the words "New Negro" appeared in the name of Winfield's dance company. The term, frequently used by Marcus Garvey, had been in general currency since the early 1920s and had been consecrated in the title and the title essay of Alain Locke's compendium *The New Negro* in 1925.

Though strict demarcation of one period from another would decree that the Harlem Renaissance ended with the onset of the 1930s, the tradition of events, recitals and serious soul-searching forums character-istic of that period did not. A distinctive challenge had been given to the Black artist by Langston Hughes, in his much-quoted 1926 essay "The Negro Artist and the Racial Mountain":

> Certainly there is, for the American Negro artist who can escape the restrictions the more advanced among his own group would put upon him, a great field of unused material ready for his art. Without going outside his race, and even among the better classes with their "white" culture and conscious American manners, but still Negro enough to be different, there is sufficient matter to furnish a black artist with a lifetime of creative work. And when he chooses to touch on the relations between Negroes and whites in this country, with their innumerable overtones and undertones, surely, and especially for literature and drama, there is an inexhaustible supply of themes at hand.

Writing in 1926, Alain Locke (widely hailed as the godfather or mentor of the New Negro in the Harlem Renaissance) had mused:

> But the real mine of Negro dramatic art and talent is in the subsoil of the vaudeville stage, gleaming through its slag and dross in the unmistakenly great dramatic gifts of a Bert Williams, a Florence

Mills or a Bill Robinson. Give Bojangles Robinson or George Stamper, pantomime dancers of genius, a Bakst or an expressionist setting; give Josephine Baker, Eddie Rector, Abbie Mitchell, or Ethel Waters a dignified medium, and they would be more than a sensation, they would be artistic revelations.

Hemsley Winfield

The Workers' Dance League forum, despite its possibly "alien" inspiration, was in the tradition of the Harlem Renaissance with a focus on the emergent new dance. At the conclusion of the forum, Winfield is quoted as having said that the discussion had given him a lot to think about. Tragically, he was dead of pneumonia three months later at the age of 27.

Hemsley Winfield's brief life is, however, fraught with interest. The son of Osborn and Jeraldine Hemsley Winfield, who was a playwright, his Broadway career had begun in 1926 as a member of the cast of *Lulu Belle*, one of several important plays with Black subjects (such as *Porgy* and *Scarlet Sister Mary*) by white playwrights which held the stage in the 1920s. In 1929 he appeared in the Broadway play *Harlem*, by the Black playwright Wallace Thurman (censured by some for its house rent party "slow drag" number), as well as in his mother's *Wade in the Water*. But his transition to the dance was in part due to the accident of having to stand in for an *actress* scheduled to perform in Oscar Wilde's *Salome* at the Cherry Lane Theatre. An unnamed correspondent of the *Chicago Defender* reported in its pages on July 27, 1929:

> Dressed, as it were, in an old bead portiere and nothing else to speak [of], Hemsley Winfield, America's "foremost Negro Actor" has come down from Harlem and is giving Oscar Wilde's "Salome" more than is coming to her. . . . Not since Bert Savoy was struck by lightning and Julian Eltinge retired to private life has a female impersonator impersonated with so much energy.

It is not clear how much formal dance training Hemsley Winfield had; it is very likely that he studied with Ella Gordon, who had a studio in Harlem from 1922. He almost certainly had lessons (private?) with Mikhail Mordkin, the distinguished Russian dancer who had begun to teach in New York following his American tour in 1924. His natural talents were widely acknowledged. In February 1932, together with members of his group, he appeared at the Roxy Theater in New York, in a show segment *Let Freedom Ring*, along with the Hall Johnson Choir, already noted for its work in a Broadway hit, the 1930 Pulitzer Prize-winning play, *The Green Pastures*. John Martin, reviewing in the *New York Times* of February 14, speaks of two "temptations" to be faced by the Negro artist, that of copying "the white man's art" and that of giving "the white man what he chooses to believe is Negro art." Martin goes on to say,

> Both these difficulties have been faced boldly by Mr. Winfield and his associates. They have resolutely turned their backs upon the easy device of being so many darkskinned reproductions of famous white prototypes, obtaining thereby perhaps a season's notice as a novelty and risking subsequent oblivion. They have also steadfastly refused to associate themselves with the amusement business of Harlem, where the Negro with his proverbial good nature presents

himself as what the white amusement seekers like to think he is.

The group is composed entirely of professional people – actors who have appeared in such Broadway productions as "Lulu Belle" and "Harlem," and who know the value of training and the necessity of professional discipline. There is, in short, nothing of dilettanteism about the idea or its manner of execution. Technical classes are held for physical development; and, besides the regular rehearsals, there are as many performances of one sort or another as can be managed for the sake of building group efficiency.

Though Martin found the work before him "crude," he stated:

The many effective moments in his compositions to date give reliable evidence that he will eventually work his way out to a satisfactory conclusion. At any rate, it is an effort well worth the making, and one that will be watched with interest by all who are alive to the tendencies of contemporary dancing.

The outstanding performance of Winfield's career was undoubtedly his dancing of the witch-doctor's role in the Metropolitan Opera's presentation of Louis Gruenberg's *The Emperor Jones* in 1933. The opera, billed as a jazz opera, was based by the Russian-born composer on Eugene O'Neill's celebrated play, which had often been repeated since it was first put on at the Provincetown Playhouse in 1921. Charles Gilpin had created the title role, but in the public mind it was the actor-singer Paul Robeson who was most closely associated with it, and there was speculation when the Metropolitan announced the opera that Robeson might even be asked to sing the lead. In fact, it was to be over two decades before an acknowledged Black singer would appear at the Metropolitan. However, the Metropolitan management quailed at the prospect of putting its entire corps de ballet in blackface. Accordingly, Hemsley Winfield and the New Negro Art Theater Dance Group were engaged for the opera, and critical reception of the opera's premiere focused as much on the frenzied "jungle" dancing in the opera's second and final acts as it did on the singing.

Edna Guy

In 1931 and 1932, Hemsley Winfield and his group appeared on several occasions on programs with Edna Guy. One of these on April 29, 1931 was billed as the "First Negro Dance Recital in America," conveniently overlooking a recital a month or so earlier by substantially the same group in Yonkers (though this may have been by way of a dress rehearsal). John Martin's review of the program in the next day's *New York Times* stated:

Miss Guy, who has been for some time a pupil and protegee of Ruth St. Denis, on this occasion presented two solos out of the Denishawn repertoire. One was the "Figure From Angkor-Vat," which Miss St. Denis often has danced delightfully herself, and the other a "Temple Offering" of more conventional type. The contrast in styles between the two dancers was, of course, marked, but Miss Guy none the less acquitted herself commendably. Mr. Winfield was less successful in his solo, "Bronze Study," which proved to be merely the exhibition of an exemplary physique. It is not in these dances which echo and

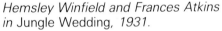

Hemsley Winfield and Frances Atkins in Jungle Wedding, *1931.*

imitate the manner of the dancers of another race that the Negro dancers are at their best, but in those in which their forthrightness and simplicity have full play. Miss Guy's group of ''spirituals'' and the primitive ritual dances by the group can be counted in this category.

While Edna Guy performed as a solo artist at the ''First Negro Dance Recital,'' and while she frequently appeared in her solo pieces in the years following, she also appeared with groups she organized, in 1932 and in 1933. Her 1933 program was held at the Harlem YWCA where her concert group performed a piece called *Woodcut Figurines*; the program included a talk by Ruth St. Denis on ''Dance as Art,'' which also praised Miss Guy for ''the afternoon's performance and for her talent for dancing,'' according to the *Amsterdam News* of May 31. Two prominent personalities of the Harlem community were involved in the program, Ivie Jackman as a dancer, and Pearl Fisher as chairlady.

Edna Guy's activities in dance continued through the 1930s, and she was one of those who welcomed Katherine Dunham to New York in 1937.

Broadway Shows, 1921–4

A single show title, *Shuffle Along*, has come to symbolize the excitement of the Black musical of the 1920s. It was the accumulation of talent which was the real strength of the production. Bordman gives this background:

> The show had been put together after a chance meeting in Philadel-phia by two black teams, Noble Sissle and Eubie Blake (for lyrics and music) and Flournoy Miller and Aubrey Lyles (for libretto). . . . For costumes they purchased clothes from a folded show. . . . The scenery was minimal. By hook or crook the company managed a series of one-night stands in New Jersey and Pennsylvania, always a step or two ahead of foreclosure, until it was felt the show was ready for New York.

Shuffle Along opened in New York on May 23, 1921, and though at first it met with indifference from the white public, it held on and slowly built up a following.

The singing and dancing in *Shuffle Along* set a Broadway standard, and despite its modest and disappointing beginnings the show ran for 504 performances on Broadway. Touring companies were formed, and it reached equal success on the extensive touring circuits of the day. Among the talents launched by the show were those of two singer-dancers: Florence Mills and Josephine Baker.

Throughout the 1920s there were repeated attempts by both Black and white producers to recapture *Shuffle Along*'s hard-earned magic with all-Black shows. Most were unsuccessful. Despite its excellent dancing, *Strut Miss Lizzie* lasted only four weeks in June of 1922. Also in June there followed *Plantation Revue*, in which Florence Mills again appeared, now with her husband, U.S. ''Slow Kid'' Thompson, who was an excellent tap-dancer. Its success was no greater, though much dancing – buck and wing, tap, and cakewalk – was in evidence. *Liza*, however, in November came closer to the mark and it was here that the first whiff of the Charleston, the dance craze of the 1920s, blew over Broadway. It was to

Ulysses ''Slow Kid'' Thompson, 1924.

The 1923 musical comedy, How Come, *featured the strutting act of Chappelle and Stinnette, and the buck and wing dancer Johnny Nit.*

be *Runnin' Wild*, however, which opened in October 1923, that would assume the mantle of *Shuffle Along*. The song "The Charleston" (composed by James P. Johnson) and its accompanying dance, became the signature of the Jazz Age.

In 1924 the shows which confirmed the talents of Josephine Baker and Florence Mills, *The Chocolate Dandies* and *Dixie to Broadway*, were both produced. Noble Sissle and Eubie Blake, who were considered the architects of the success of *Shuffle Along*, were the producers of *The*

Chocolate Dandies. The show was an expensive and lavish one, which is probably what sank it. But an unexpected star emerged from the show: the eighteen-year-old clowning chorus girl from a *Shuffle Along* road company, Josephine Baker. Her triumph was as a blackface loose-legged comic dancer. *Dixie to Broadway* emerged from *Plantation Revue*, by way of a tour in England, and presented Florence Mills in a showstopping number, "Jungle Nights in Dixieland."

After these two shows there were no Black musicals on Broadway for three years, except for a stereotypical *Lucky Sambo* in 1925.

Florence Mills

Florence Mills had begun her career as a child singer and dancer and was a polished performer by the time of her appearance in *Shuffle Along* when she was widely applauded. While in *Shuffle Along*, she was lured, along with her husband, to Lew Leslie's Plantation Club; there she eventually became the star of the revue named for the club. Leslie took the revue to England where it was attached back to back to an English revue and toured as *Dover to Dixie*; this in turn he brought to New York as *Dixie to Broadway*, which was to be the last appearance of Florence Mills on Broadway.

During the period when there were no Black musicals on Broadway, a hiatus caused by a shortage of theaters (the mid-1920s was the busiest period in the history of Broadway: it has been downhill ever since) and by racial prejudice, Leslie booked his next show, *Blackbirds*, which starred Florence Mills, into the Alhambra Theater in Harlem where it was a ringing success, making Mills the undisputed favorite of the Black Mecca. The show then went to Paris, and to London, with Mills being acclaimed in both cities. She returned to New York, where she died suddenly in the summer of 1927, after a routine appendectomy.

In what did the magic of Florence Mills consist? In *The Seven Lively Arts* (1924), Gilbert Seldes proclaimed:

> ... to watch her walk out upon the stage with her long free stride and her superb, shameless swing, is an aesthetic pleasure; two other

The Chocolate Dandies, *1924.*

Florence Mills, Dixie to Broadway, *1924.*

actors I have seen so take a chance; Cohan by stage instinct, Marie Tempest by a cultivated genius. Florence Mills is almost the definition of the romantic *une force qui va*, but she remains an original, with little or nothing to give beyond her presence, her instinctive grace, and her baffling, seductive voice.

Three decades later Seldes commented, in a reissue of his book, on his earlier enthusiasm:

> And Florence Mills, who died very young, is after all these years, a great person in the memory of all who saw her. A European composer, seeing her offstage, said to me, "This is the first aristocrat I've seen in America," and called attention to the fragile wrists and ankles, the delicacy of her entire form, the enlightened gaiety of her expression.

Seldes's observations explain Buddy Bradley's remark, on meeting Alicia Markova, that she reminded him of Florence Mills.

Josephine Baker

Whereas Florence Mills was usually characterized as ethereal, Josephine Baker – both in her original comic persona and in the primitive persona which she assumed in Europe – was "earthereal." After her appearance in *The Chocolate Dandies*, she was hired as one of the cast in a Black show being organized for Paris by a white woman producer. The show, opening at the prestigious Théâtre des Champs-Elysées in Paris on October 20, 1925 as the *Revue Nègre*, became the rage of the Paris season and went on to tour other European capitals, including Berlin. Everywhere Josephine Baker, featured as a scantily-clad jungle princess dancing to the beat of the tom-tom, was idolized and lionized. Her triumph was instantaneous, her talent obviously great, and her gift for assimilation and improvisation phenomenal.

The Russian-born André Levinson (considered to be France's first modern dance critic, as Carl Van Vechten is considered to be America's) said of Baker at her appearance in Paris, after remarking that normally "the dancer follows the musical text,"

> With Miss Josephine Baker, all seems to change. It is she, with her frenzied fluttering, her bold isolations, her thrusting movements, who projects the rhythmic flow. She seems to dictate to the entranced drummer, to the saxophonist straining soulfully toward her. . . . The music is born of the dance and what a dance! . . . The plastic sense of a race of sculptors and the fury of the African Eros engage us.

Hairstyles, clothing, perfumes, were all launched under her name and image. Following the *Revue Nègre*, she went to the Folies Bergère and, after a tour which included Eastern Europe and South America, she became the star of a show at the Casino de Paris.

Josephine Baker had arrived in Paris at a moment when, with no concern at all for historical and cultural accuracy, the French avant garde, following artists in various mediums, was enthusiastic about African art and Black American jazz, and smitten with self-congratulation over its colonies in the Caribbean and elsewhere. She inherited and concentrated all of this aesthetic sensation for a prestigious public. Her sharp native

Josephine Baker, about 1926.

29

- Kingston Sixth Form Centre LIBRARY

Poster for Josephine Baker at the Folies Bergère.

Poster for Josephine Baker's final show in Paris in 1975; she was 68.

AVEC LE CONCOURS DE ... MONTE-CARLO
BOBINO
JEAN-CLAUDE DAUZONNE présente
festival
EXCLUSIVITE
MUSIDISC
EUROPE
UN GRAND SPECTACLE DE
ANDRE LEVASSEUR
Josephine

intelligence, her appreciation of acclaim, and the alacrity with which she, an untutored American, became a cultivated Frenchwoman, enabled her to achieve and maintain a position of eminence (although, after a few years, she was no longer primarily a dancer).

Josephine Baker appeared in the United States again in the mid-1930s, after she had become the feted singing star of the Paris music hall, known for the elegance of her costume on and off stage. She had made a film, *Zouzou*, and appeared in an Offenbach opera, *La Créole*. Among the performers in the *Ziegfeld Follies* of 1936, produced by the Shuberts at the Winter Garden, were Fanny Brice, Gertrude Niesen, Eve Arden, Judy Canova, and Bob Hope. Josephine appeared in a production number entitled, predictably, "Island in the West Indies." It is not clear whether George Balanchine, one of the choreographers of the show, was involved with this number, though he certainly remembered Baker from his Paris days. Her appearance was not a triumph.

Josephine Baker in America, 1964.

Dance Hall and Nightclub

The dance hall and the prohibition-defying nightclub existed in many of America's large urban centers during the 1920s. Both continued in vigorous life until World War II, and a few survived much longer. It is a measure of the dominance of Black dance in the American consciousness that, looking back, the most memorable of these institutions were both in Harlem: the Savoy Ballroom and the Cotton Club. Both were owned by whites, and the latter catered almost exclusively to whites, but because of their music and dance components they were perceived as quintessentially Black. The Savoy was for the masses, and the Cotton Club for the fun-seeking big spenders.

Harlem had other dance halls, notably the Renaissance, and white New York had Roseland and many others. They existed in other cities. In Philadelphia, for example, a white dance hall, Dreamland, reserved Thursdays for Blacks, dubbing itself Shadowland for that evening. Dance halls ranged from the opulent to the squalid. But the Savoy, "the home of happy feet," epitomizes them.

Opened in 1921, the Savoy was to have a lifespan of 33 years, closing in a rather decayed state in 1954. During its long life 250 different dance bands played for its patrons, some of whom came nearly every night, though the cognoscenti regarded the nights of the week as belonging to different groups. Monday was ladies' night, Tuesday was for serious dancers, Wednesday and Friday was when clubs and fraternal organizations came, Thursday was for domestics (the so-called "kitchen mechanics"), Saturday was "squares' night" and Sunday "celebrities' night."

At the Savoy, the northeast corner of the dance floor came to be known at the Cats' Corner, where the virtuosic dancers disported themselves and excluded others. Here were seen the most exciting variations of the Lindy Hop in the 1930s or jitterbugging in the 1940s, dances whose basic character long preceded the opening of the Savoy and which continued to be developed there and elsewhere by generations of dancers down to the close of the dance halls, and the replacement of couple dancing by the solo varieties which became the basis of disco dancing.

In the 1930s many of the Savoy's resident dancers became well-known in Harlem and elsewhere. Among these were Leon James, Shorty

Norton and Margot were a ballroom
team in the years 1933–47.

Leon James and Willa Mae Ricker
Lindy-Hopping, 1941.

Snowden and Big Bea, and Stretch Jones and Little Bea, who specialized
in so-called floor steps. Younger dancers, who refined the "air" steps,
included Al Minns and Pepsi Bethel. The dancing of some of these
performers was captured at the Savoy in the 1940s on silent film by Mura
Dehn, a Russian-born modern dancer of the 1930s. An edited version
with dubbed music, *The Spirit Moves*, has been released. For several years
Mura Dehn directed the Traditional Jazz Dance Company, composed of
Savoy dancers. Studio shots of these dancers are included in the film.

The Cotton Club, whose story has been hinted at in films, has also been
the subject of a book by Jim Haskins. Coming into existence in 1923 at
142nd Street and Lenox Avenue, in a space previously used by boxer
Jack Johnson for his unsuccessful Club Delux, it was well financed – by
crime syndicate money. (Small's Paradise, which was to have a parallel

but less brilliant history, was also opened in 1923.) The Cotton Club exploited and fostered the primitive or jungle motif which afflicted Black performers in the 1920s and later. The signature band from December 1927 to the end of the Harlem period was first known as "Duke Ellington's Jungle Band."

The Cotton Club revues, originally staged by the ubiquitous Lew Leslie, were sumptuous and pace-setting, featuring high-stepping chorus girls and specialty dancers. From 1931 on, they were usually set by the Black dance director Clarence Robinson. By this time the Cab Calloway band frequently alternated with that of Duke Ellington. Songs were usually provided by white composers and lyricists, including Harold Arlen, a master of Black style.

One of the most famous of the specialty dance acts was that of Earl "Snake Hips" Tucker. Though much imitated, he was apparently never equaled. In their account of American vernacular dance, *Jazz Dance*, Marshall and Jean Stearns graphically recount his routine and the complex audience response he elicited.

The Harlem Cotton Club was closed in February 1936 and in September the downtown Cotton Club opened its doors, closing in June 1940. The downtown opening show, staged by Clarence Robinson, featured Bill Robinson and the Bahama dancers, with music by Cab Calloway's

Henri Wessels and Anice Boyer, specialty act, Cotton Club parade, 1929–30, dances staged by Elida Webb.

The Berry Brothers, one of the great "flash" acts, who appeared with Bill Robinson at the opening of the Cotton Club Downtown, 1936.

Maude Russell and her Ebony Steppers.

Orchestra. A 1937 show featured the Nicholas Brothers, and Bill Bailey, as well as the Duke Ellington Orchestra.

Perhaps one of the most enduring spillovers of the tradition represented by the Harlem Cotton Club were the summer spectaculars by the show director Larry Steele at the Club Harlem in Atlantic City, which continued down through the 1950s.

Vaudeville and Tap

The 1920s saw the height of the vaudeville or variety stage show tradition in the United States. Vaudeville houses were still to be found coast to coast, in big cities and small towns, and hosts of performers, in a sense descendants of the nineteenth-century minstrels, white and Black, were busy year-round supplying entertainment. The prescient saw in the popularity of the film an encroachment, but not until the commercialization of the sound film, prophetically announced by *The Jazz Singer*, a film in which Al Jolson did his time-honored blackface routine, and which had its premiere on October 6, 1927, was the writing clearly on the wall. In the 1930s the musical film, aided by the Depression, rapidly superseded vaudeville. The last refuge of vaudeville was the Black community, which held on to its major houses such as the Apollo in New York, the Royal in Baltimore, and the Howard in Washington until the beginning of the 1960s.

Tap-dancing was the highlight of the vaudeville repertory in the 1920s and was to survive into the age of the Hollywood musical as an indispensable ingredient for the audience's pleasure. Several great Black tap-dancers either emerged to fame in the 1920s or began their careers then; their style was a direct descendant of that of King Rastus Brown. His technique seems to have developed from shuffle dancing of the Minstrel period, and his rhythmic pedal counterpoint to standard time was infinitely varied. Such terms as "buck dancing" and "time step" came to be used to describe different aspects of the technique of King Rastus Brown, who flourished in the period 1906–10, and whose dancing career apparently ended before 1920.

Younger contemporaries of his who were celebrated in the 1920s include U.S. "Slow Kid" Thompson (husband of Florence Mills and frequently billed with her), Eddie Rector, and Bill "Bojangles" Robinson. This decade saw the rise of one of the stellar Black tap performers, John Bubbles (John Sublett) who was to be known both as a solo artist and in the team of Buck and Bubbles, with Ford Lee Washington. Buck and Bubbles were sensations of the *Ziegfeld Follies of 1931*. Also to be numbered among Black tap-dancers who emerged at that time is Bill Bailey (brother of Pearl Bailey).

Black Musicals, 1927–8

The Black musical tumbled back on to Broadway in June 1927 with a piece called *Bottomland*, dismissed as being both stereotypical and flawed with imitations of whites. *The New York Times* admonished, "Pickaninnies are not ladies of the ensemble." A few weeks later a show gratuitously called *Africana* presented an ebullient Ethel Waters, at that time more praised for her dancing than for her singing and often compared to the white dancing comedienne Charlotte Greenwood. Hard upon that came *Rang Tang*, whose jungle choreography found favor.

The next year, Miller and Lyles made an attempt to recapture the magic of *Shuffle Along* in a piece called *Keep Shufflin'*, with songs by Fats Waller, and lyrics by Andy Razaf. The dancing was reported as so energetic as to knock the show out of line. The production was a moderate success.

The great success of 1928, however, was *Blackbirds of 1928*. The original *Blackbirds* (1926) had not been seen by Broadway. After its reign in Harlem, it decamped for the conquest of Paris and London. It was planned to bring the new version to Broadway with its international star, Florence Mills. Her death interposed. Instead, the production opened, acquired Bill Robinson, became a sensation and ran for 518 performances.

Bill "Bojangles" Robinson

Bill Robinson had appeared at New York's major vaudeville house, the Palace, as early as 1921, and from 1926 to 1932 he was a consistent Palace headliner. His long apprenticeship was capped by his triumphant appearance in *Blackbirds of 1928*, a show which he made a hit, when he was 50. He was the star of two further Broadway shows, *Brown Buddies* (1930), a moderate success, and *Blackbirds of 1933*, a victim of the Depression. In 1930 he made a Hollywood musical, *Dixiana*, set in an incongruous New Orleans of the 1840s, and 1932 saw him in the all-Black New York film *Harlem is Heaven*, which also featured Eubie Blake. He went on in the mid-1930s to become a Hollywood movie star appearing in 14 films.

Bill "Bojangles" Robinson's singing and dancing in Blackbirds of 1928 *made him "one of the great artists of the modern stage."*

Buck and Bubbles, 1930. John Bubbles was called the master of rhythm tap.

Carl Van Vechten says of Robinson:

> He tapped not only with his nimble feet, but also enlisted, with electrifying results, the aid of both hands, both expressive eyes, his mobile torso, and even his hat, which appeared to have a life of its own, in his brilliant exhibition.

The Stearns state it more soberly:

> Bill Robinson's contribution to tap dancing is exact and specific: He brought it up on the toes, dancing upright and swinging. . . . The flat-footed wizardry of King Rastus Brown, although some old-timers still prefer it, seemed earthbound compared to the tasty steps of Bojangles who danced with a hitherto-unknown lightness and presence.

Buddy Bradley and Black Dance Directors

A white revue, *The Little Show*, created three new stars in April 1929: Fred Allen, Clifton Webb and Libby Holman. The number which sealed the success of the latter two, "Moanin' Low," was drawn from the imagery of Black low-life; sung by Holman, it was danced by Webb in steps inspired by "Snake Hips" Tucker of the Cotton Club. This dance, called "High

Yaller," was diffused with diagrams and illustrations in a magazine, *The Dance*. It had been choreographed by a Black dance coach, Buddy Bradley, a fact that Webb had forgotten some years later when he remembered his own creation of the dance.

In *Jazz Dance*, Marshall and Jean Stearns recount the story of Buddy Bradley at some length. Among the white dancers whom he coached and prepared routines for, according to the Stearns, were Mae West, Ed Wynn, Golda Gray, Eddie Fay, Ruby Keeler, Adele and Fred Astaire, Lucille Ball, Eleanor Powell, and Paul Draper. In 1928 Billy Pierce, a Black entrepreneur, opened a dance studio on West 46th Street, specifically to provide a place where white performers could learn Black routines from Black coaches. Newspaper accounts of the day usually identify Pierce as a dancing master, but in fact he was simply a middleman for dance professionals such as Bradley. Bradley's first great success was with the *Greenwich Village Follies of 1928*, which was originally choreographed by Busby Berkeley. The producer, Morris Green, had Bradley re-choreograph the entire production, though Berkeley's name still figured on the program and Bradley was unmentioned.

The standard method of white dance directors – the term "choreographer" entered the Broadway vocabulary with George Balanchine – when working with Black performers was to allow them to do whatever they wanted to do. Lew Leslie of *Blackbirds* fame was a successful exploiter of this procedure. It was the English producer, Charles Cochrane, who, in taking over the British production of *Blackbirds*, hired Buddy Bradley as dance director and gave him credit for his work. In 1933 Bradley joined Cochrane in England to choreograph *Evergreen*. Thereafter he remained in England. In 1935 he choreographed the film version of *Evergreen* and *Radio Parade* of 1935. In 1936 he choreographed the film *It's Love Again* and as late as 1946 another film, *Walking on Air*, featuring Black skaters and a Black ballerina. However, he worked mainly on stage shows in France, Italy, and Spain, as well as in England, collaborating with figures such as Anton Dolin, Frederick Ashton, and Leonide Massine from the world of ballet, and coaching Alicia Markova, among others.

Bradley was succeeded at the Pierce Studio by Herbie Harper, who later worked on the first production of *Porgy and Bess*, as well as with Balanchine on the Ray Bolger choreography for "Slaughter on Tenth Avenue" in *On Your Toes*.

Other Black dance directors named by the Stearns include Charlie Davis, Addison Davis, Sammy Dyer, Willie Covan, and Clarence Robinson.

Earl "Snake Hips" Tucker starred in Blackbirds of 1928.

Black Broadway After the Crash

In June of 1929 *Bamboola* complimented the new legendary status of Bill Robinson by imitation; no less than twenty tap-dancers did their version of the staircase routine which had become his signature. Bill Robinson himself returned to Broadway in *Brown Buddies* in October 1930, while a few weeks later Lew Leslie in a 1930 version of *Blackbirds* featured Buck and Bubbles, as well as Ethel Waters. The dancing team Chilton and Thomas was featured in Al Jolson's cafe-style *Wonder Bar* in 1931. Jolson, eschewing blackface and basking in his new Hollywood-based fame, impersonated the master of ceremonies of a Parisian club. He introduced

Carroll Chilton and Maceo Thomas, husband and wife, as the greatest dancing team in the world. The couple had indeed created a furor in England the previous year and had appeared at a command performance there. They continued in vaudeville for a few years thereafter.

In September 1931, *Fast and Furious* presented skits and dancing and *Singin' the Blues* gave greater importance to the dance with staging by the white dance director Sammy Lee. *Sugar Hill* in December was an unsuccessful attempt by Miller and Lyles to find once again the magic of *Shuffle Along*. Undeterred by this failure they tried again a year later with *Shuffle Along of 1932*; while the dancing received some praise, the circumstances of the Depression were reflected in a reduced corps of dancers. The demise of the Black musical genre which had been characteristic of the 1920s on Broadway, uptown in Harlem at the Lafayette and the Alhambra, and on the road, was made clear by the fate of Lew Leslie's *Blackbirds of 1933*. Even with Bill Robinson, it lasted only three weeks. An era had ended. Prohibition was repealed. Robinson went to Hollywood.

Black Material in Denishawn and in the New Dance

Ruth St. Denis has been quoted as saying, "The Negro is our real dancing teacher. To him it is a vital and necessary thing to dance." Early Denishawn reflected the sentiment not at all. In 1921, however, Ted Shawn choreographed *Juba*, to a composition of the Black American composer R. Nathaniel Dett. Designed for three dancers, it was danced by Martha Graham, among others, in Shawn's small group tour of 1921. In 1923, to a piece by the New Orleans-born composer Louis Moreau Gottschalk, he composed *Pasquinade* (also sometimes known as "A Creole Belle"). It is not absolutely clear whether this piece, danced by Doris Humphrey, was intended overtly to reflect the Black experience, but the overtones are there. There can be little doubt, however, that Shawn's *Crapshooter* of 1925, danced by Charles Weidman, was so intended. Both *Pasquinade* and *Crapshooter* were performed on the Denishawn tour to the Far East.

In 1931, the last year in which Denishawn formally existed, Shawn included in *Four Dances Based on American Folk Music*, which he danced himself, a dance simply titled "Negro Spiritual." In 1933 began the seven-year career of Ted Shawn and his Men Dancers. For the first season's repertory of the all-male company, with its strong emphasis on Native American and folk traditions, Shawn repeated his American Folk Dance solos and choreographed a group piece, *Negro Spirituals I* ("Go Down, Moses"; "Jacob's Ladder") in which Barton Mumaw and Jack Cole (I. Ewing Cole) both appeared; for the second season Shawn choreographed *Negro Spirituals II* ("Nobody Knows the Trouble I See"; "Go Down, Moses"; and "Swing Low, Sweet Chariot"). Shawn later created two pieces of Black inspiration: *Danza Afro-Cubana* (1935) to music of Ernesto Lecuona and *Jazz Decade* as the climax to his full evening piece *O, Libertad!* (1937).

Shawn had already been anticipated in his use of Black material by Helen Tamiris who in 1928, in her second solo concert, included *Two Negro Spirituals* ("Nobody Knows de Trouble I See"; "Joshua Fit de Battle ob Jericho"). Her success in these pieces, which she performed in Paris and Berlin, subsequently led her to augment them by a version of "Swing Low, Sweet Chariot" on her triumphant return program in New York in

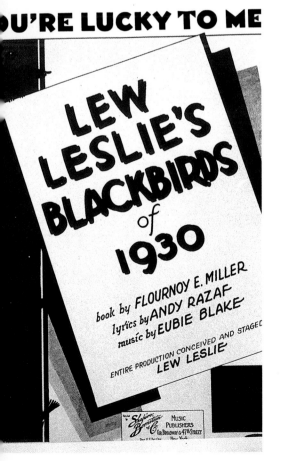

Lew Leslie's Blackbirds of 1930 *featured Ethel Waters, the Berry Brothers, and Buck and Bubbles.*

April 1929. The program included also *Popular Rhythms* to music of W. C. Handy ("Father of the Blues"), which did not survive to be included in the program's repetition "by popular demand" a week later. The spirituals, which expanded in number in later programs, became in fact the signature pieces of Tamiris's art. Of her the critic Margaret Lloyd said, "The Negro Spirituals were the musts of her programs. Every new one was hailed with hurrahs. This was the thing she could really do, this was what she did best."

For her spirituals, Tamiris used the arrangements of J. Rosamond Johnson and Laurence Brown, then much favored. In a recital in December, 1932 she danced six Negro spirituals, as well as a *Gris-Gris Ceremonial* to the percussive rhythms of gourds. The dance was one supposedly based on a ritual of West African origin in which the "gris-gris," a fetish figure, is propitiated in the forest. The following summer she appeared in Lewisohn Stadium in the famed outdoor concert season of the Philharmonic Orchestra with a group of Bahama Negro Dancers, performing *Gris-Gris Ceremonial* with the dancers and accompanied by "gourds and orchestra."

Of Esther Jungen, another pioneer in the new dance, Margaret Lloyd says:

> Esther made a triumphal entrance into the concert field at the Guild Theatre on November 23, 1930. Her first major work, *Go Down Death*, from James Weldon Johnson's *God's Trombones*, was an immediate success. The poet himself read the lines and Esther danced in a neo-primitive style to which she later largely adhered.

In 1932 Jungen repeated *Go Down Death* with the poem being read by Richard B. Harrison, an eminent Black Shakespearean elocutionist, then something of a celebrity after playing God in *The Green Pastures*.

The Bahamian Connection

An unsuccessful Black revue that played a forlorn week on Broadway in September 1931 was *Fast and Furious*. The anthropological folklorist Zora Neale Hurston, who had been one of the bright literary talents of the Harlem Renaissance and who was later to attain distinction as a novelist, had indulged her theatrical ambitions by contributing three sketches to *Fast and Furious*, after a previous abortive collaboration with Langston Hughes on a folk drama, *Mule Bone*. Not only did Hurston write sketches for the revue, but she appeared in a cheerleader's scene along with Jackie Mabley, the comedienne. Hurston had approached Hall Johnson, whose choir in *The Green Pastures* had been a great success, about a collaboration of some sort. Her potential performers included a group of Bahamians from the island of Bimini, who had already acquired some reputation as performers. The production, intended to present a folkloric interpretation of a day in the life of railroad builders, did not ultimately enlist Johnson's support, though (according to Hurston's biographer, Robert Hemenway) Hurston asserted correctly that Johnson appropriated some of her ideas for his *Run Little Chillun*.

The Hurston production *Great Day*, produced with borrowed funds, did have a one-performance *succès d'estime* on January 10, 1932, but for a variety of reasons had no further theatrical presentation. A concert performance of some of the material was presented in March of the same

Coles and Atkins, 1946, known as "the last of the class acts."

Posters for Run, Little Chillun, *1933.*

year. There was later some acrimony involving the dancers, who claimed that money was due to them.

In the winter of 1932, Hall Johnson was working on his *Run Little Chillun*, and he secured the services of the Bahamian dancers. He asked Doris Humphrey, then pregnant, to stage their performance. Humphrey was ultimately unsatisfied with the assignment, finding the dancers interesting but Johnson tedious in his insistence on minimizing their work so that "his rather heavy and sanctimonious drama may proceed." Humphrey wrote an article about the Bahamian dancers which appeared in *American Dancer* in July, 1933.

The next appearance of the Bahamian dancers was with Tamiris in the Lewisohn Stadium concert; there they performed the following dances, presumably from their basic repertoire: "Dance of the Coconut Grove," "Congo," "The Jumpin' Dance," "The Fire Dance."

A group of Bahamian dancers is listed as appearing on the Variety and Theater program of the National Dance Congress on May 24, 1936. These were probably the same dancers who were in the lineup at the opening show of the downtown Cotton Club in September of the same year.

Bill Robinson and Lena Horne in the film Stormy Weather, *1943.*

3

The Expanding World of Dance

*A*fter the inauguration of Franklin D. Roosevelt in 1933, the New Deal began taking shape immediately as a response to the Great Depression. One aspect of the New Deal program, which was to mark a considerable innovation in the United States government's relationship to the arts, was the inclusion of artists and writers among the classes of the unemployed to be put to work. An outcome of this was the Federal Theatre Project of the Works Progress Administration (WPA), and its associated dance activities in which many choreographers and dancers were involved. The various Federal arts programs included Black participants in many areas.

The "new" American concert dance which had emerged in the 1920s was definitively baptized "the modern dance" by John Martin, whom *The New York Times* had appointed in 1927 as the first full-time dance critic in the United States. His book, *The Modern Dance*, was published in 1933, and in the same year Ted Shawn formed his all-male dance company. The next year, two events occurred which were crucial to the modern dance: the creation of the Bennington College Summer School, and the initiation of the dance concert series at the Young Men's Hebrew Association (YMHA; later YM-YWHA) Auditorium on 92nd Street in Manhattan.

By 1934 the pioneers of the previous decade – Graham, Humphrey, and Weidman – were busily teaching, refining their art, and creating dance compositions. Tamiris, never associated with Bennington as were the other three, was to begin a close association with the Federal Theatre and with its political consciousness. She continued to utilize themes and music of Black America in her work.

The Dance International Program of 1937 saw the participation of all the aforementioned dancers, as well as of Ruth St. Denis and Hanya Holm. Holm had come to the United States in the early 1930s to establish a school whose curriculum was based on the art of the German modern dance pioneer, Mary Wigman, but she had modified her program in response to the American environment and in reaction to political events in Germany.

In 1940, Ted Shawn, having disbanded his all-male dance company, established the Jacob's Pillow Dance Festival whose importance to the whole realm of concert-theatrical dance, as well as to Black dancers, was to be considerable. In 1942, largely in response to the coming of World War II, the Bennington Summer School ceased operations.

Broadway underwent a considerable transformation between 1933 and 1945 in terms of the musical theater and of dance. The crash of 1929 had cast a pall on venturesomeness, and the flurry of Black shows which had appeared from 1927 onward ground to a halt in 1933. The Swing Era of the 1930s did little for Black dancers, except on the vaudeville stage and in film. The Federal Theatre, however, provided opportunities, including the earliest apparent assaults on racial segregation. The success of Katherine Dunham on Broadway in 1940 modified the status of the Black dancer there, and – since she came from the concert-theatrical tradition – she had an impact on dancers in that mode as well.

The opening of the School of American Ballet in 1934 under the supervision of the newly-arrived George Balanchine was rich with consequences for the development of American ballet. That same year Catherine Littlefield created the Philadelphia Ballet, and Ruth Page became the prima ballerina and choreographer for the Chicago Civic Opera. By the next year, Balanchine and Lincoln Kirstein had created the American Ballet, the first of a series of companies which culminated in the formation of the New York City Ballet. Kirstein also published his history of the dance in 1935. In 1937 Mordkin's ballet company, which was to be the nucleus of American Ballet Theatre (ABT), came on the scene. But except for an ill-fated experiment by the German-born dancer and ballet master, Eugene Von Grona, in 1937 and the short-lived Negro wing of ABT under Agnes de Mille, by and large Blacks were not involved in ballet until after World War II.

Randolph Sawyer, Jacob's Pillow, 1942.

Black Dance in Films

The Hollywood musical of the 1930s probably brought more dance into the experience of the American public than did any other medium at that period. Thematically, there were many types of musicals, but the type which gave greatest hospitality to Black tap-dancers, the only kind of Black dance at first recognized by Hollywood, was the revue. (Several of the precocious waif films featuring Shirley Temple found a place for Bill Robinson, but as a kindly Black servitor.)

The first all-Black musical film was the 1929 MGM production *Hallelujah*, directed by King Vidor. Set in the cotton belt of the South, it utilized Black folk music effectively. At the behest of the producers, and apparently against the wishes of the director, two Irving Berlin songs were injected to give "life" to the film. One of these, "Swanee Shuffle," was the accompaniment to a dance of seduction by the beautiful lead actress Nina Mae McKinney. The 1933 filming of *The Emperor Jones*, which starred Paul Robeson, provided some glimpses of putative primitive dancing as well as of a ring shout and of cabaret dancing.

It was Bill Robinson and tap, however, which constituted the chief

Bill Robinson and chorus.

Katherine Dunham in The Woman With the Cigar *at the Windsor Theater, February 1940.*

direct Black contribution to the Hollywood musical in the 1930s. Though he had made an early appearance in the film *Dixiana* (1930), it was a series of films beginning in 1935 which made him a dancing celebrity of the film era. A number of these films presented him as a kindly servant benevolently watching over child star Shirley Temple, the dance consisting of a follow-the-leader routine featuring the elderly Black man and the tiny blonde tyke. The Robinson-Temple collaboration included the "Stair Dance" in *The Little Colonel* and "Polly Wolly Doodle" in *The Littlest Rebel* (both 1935), *Dimples* (1936), "Parade of the Wooden Soldiers" in *Rebecca of Sunnybrook Farm* and "I Love to Walk in the Rain" in *Just Across the Corner* (both 1938). By the last of these Shirley Temple's popularity was already on the wane, and Robinson was 60.

Other Robinson films were *Hooray for Love* (1935), *The Big Broadcast of 1936* (1935), in which the Nicholas Brothers also appeared, *The Hit Parade* (1937), *One Mile From Heaven* (1937), *In Old Kentucky* (1937) and *Up the River* (1938). There was a hiatus of five years, before Robinson appeared in the star-studded *Stormy Weather* (1943).

Fredi Washington, best known as a dramatic actress and celebrated for her role of the "tragic mulatto" in the first film version of *Imitation of Life*,

Poster for Porgy and Bess, *which opened October 10, 1935, in New York City, with John Bubbles as Sportin' Life.*

was a dancer in the Cotton Club style, also danced in several films including *One Mile From Heaven*. The first of her dancing films had been a short, *Black and Tan* (1929). She also appeared in *Symphony in Black* (1935), which affords the only cinematic revelation of the art of Earl "Snake Hips" Tucker, accompanied by the Duke Ellington orchestra.

Bill Robinson's representation of tap in the 1930s was in no way "state of the art," but rather an urbane style he had perfected on the vaudeville circuit twenty years before. In the meantime, a highly acrobatic style of tap had emerged, and – apart from Buck and Bubbles, who were close to Robinson in style, though they used more intricate steps – most Black tap in films of this period was highly acrobatic, and virtuosic.

After an early appearance in *Darktown Follies* (1930), a Pathé two-reeler, and a night club short, *Harlem Bound*, which had a finale of the Cotton Club chorus, Buck and Bubbles appeared in *Calling All Stars*, a British film, which also included the agile Nicholas Brothers. Then Buck and Bubbles performed in four Hollywood films: *The Varsity Show* (1937), *Beauty Shoppe* (1938), a vaudeville story, *Atlantic City* (1944), and a Danny Kaye film, *A Song is Born* (1948).

Rivals for primacy in the acrobatic or "flash act" line were Fayard and Harold Nicholas, the Nicholas Brothers, and the Berry Brothers. The Nicholas Brothers were better known and had a longer career both on stage and in the movies. While a youthful Cotton Club act they appeared in a short, *Pie, Pie Blackbird* (1933), and then in the films *Kid Millions* (1934) and *The Big Broadcast of 1936* (1935). They were on stage in *Ziegfeld Follies of 1936*, followed by a stint in the English *Blackbirds*, choreographed by Buddy Bradley. While in England they appeared in the British film *Calling All Stars* (1937), which also featured Buck and Bubbles. Another stint on Broadway followed in Rodgers and Hart's *Babes in Arms*, choreographed by George Balanchine, who contributed some movements to their act.

The film career of the Nicholas Brothers, along with that of the Berry Brothers, was at its height in the 1940s. The films of the Nicholas Brothers were *Tin Pan Alley* (1940), *Down Argentine Way* (1940), *Sun Valley Serenade* (1941), *The Great American Broadcast* (1941), *Orchestra Wives* (1942), *Stormy Weather* (1943), and *The Pirates* (1948).

The films of the Berry Brothers, a trio consisting of Ananius (Nias), Jimmy, and Warren Berry, were *Lady Be Good* (1941), *Panama Hattie* (1942), *Boarding House Blues* (1948), and *You're My Everything* (1949).

Providing strong competition to both the Nicholas Brothers and the Berry Brothers were the Four Stepbrothers, a name covering shifting personnel who included Al Williams, Maceo Anderson, Red Gordon, Sherman Robinson, Sylvester Johnson, Freddie James and others. The first two were the anchor dancers. Though they made a short, *Barbershop Blues* in 1933, their main Hollywood period was in the early 1940s and is represented by the following: *When Johnny Comes Marching Home* (1942), *Rhythm of the Islands*, choreographed by Lester Horton (1943), *It Ain't Hay* (1943), *Hi Buddy* (1943), *Greenwich Village*, featuring Carmen Miranda, and *Carolina Blues*, in which Harold Nicholas also appeared (both 1944), and *Shine On, Harvest Moon* (1946). In the declining period of the Hollywood musical, the Four Stepbrothers appeared in the Bob Hope film *Here Come the Girls* (1953).

The crowning achievement of the representation of Black dance and dancers occurred in the film *Stormy Weather* (1943). The fragile plot — which involved a romance between 65-year-old Bill Robinson and the ravishing Lena Horne, then in her mid-twenties — strained Black credulity, but it allowed a revue format in which not only Robinson could dance, but so could the Katherine Dunham troupe — and the Nicholas Brothers, Lena Horne, Cab Calloway and others.

Asadata Dafora and African Dance-drama

The appearance in 1934 of an African "opera," *Kykunkor*, with its extensive use of the dance, was electrifying. Alain Locke, ever alert to new possibilities in Negro art, noted in his annual review in *Opportunity* that the creator:

> . . . has really made a contribution to the drama of the African theme and setting; only its difficult intricacies of dance, pantomime, chant and drum-orchestra technique will prevent its sweeping the Negro stage with cleansing and illuminating fire. The production should by all means have a photo-sound recording; it is a classic of a new genre and will be eventually a turning point in Negro native drama.

The author and choreographer, John Warner Dafora Horton (Asadata Dafora), was a native of Sierra Leone who had come to New York in 1929

(Above left) Alma Sutton, soloist in Kykunkor.

(Above) Asadata Dafora and Frances Atkins in Kykunkor, 1934.

at the age of 38. After having been in the British army in World War I, he had studied voice in Italy and Germany, with the hope of becoming an opera singer on the European stage. He did not achieve this, but in consequence, Horton, a man of vast culture, spoke French, Italian and German and had a sound grounding in Euro-classical music.

In his native Sierra Leone he had also had some actual contact with Mende life and culture, which was not always the case with members of the Creole elite to which his parents belonged. In New York, influenced by the aesthetic of European opera, he began working with a group of African men of various origins, residents of Harlem who frequented the National African Union (a social club), in order to try out his creative ideas. The performing group he formed, Shologa Oloba, became the vehicle for the realization of an African "opera."

In 1933 the all-male troupe performed scenes from *Zoonga*, probably a work in progress by Dafora, at the Communist Party Bazaar at Madison Square Garden. This led to an offer of a theater and the next year Shologa Oloba, augmented by Afro-American women, most of whom had no stage experience, and none of whom had any direct acquaintance with African culture, presented *Kykunkor* to widespread enthusiasm and applause, though Lincoln Kirstein, writing in the *Nation*, after describing sympathetically the peregrinations of *Kykunkor* from the Unity Theater to

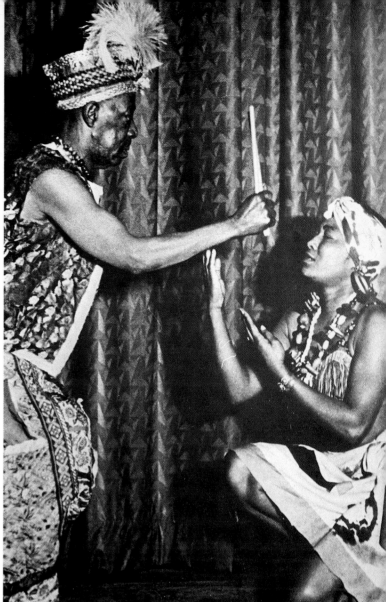

(Above) Abdul Assen as the Witch Doctor, Kykunkor.

(Above right) Asadata Dafora and Esther Rolle.

City College Auditorium, and finally the Theater in the Sky of the Chanin Building concluded: "The show is interesting, although it is neither a consistent dramatic whole, nor an 'authentic' piece of anthropology nor an 'artistic' experience."

By 1935 the group had become the African Dance Troupe of the Federal Theatre Project, and in 1936 appeared in dances arranged by Dafora in the famed voodoo *Macbeth* of Orson Welles. It appears that the Afro-American male dancer Archie Savage was also in this production. The group went on to create *Bassa Moona*, an opera on a Nigerian theme devised by two Nigerians in the company, Momodu Johnson and Norman Coker. Alain Locke was again gratified:

> . . . *Bassa Moona*, first project of the African Dance Unit, follows the promising trail of *Kykunkor* – with an African plot, setting, chants, dances and special drum orchestra music. *Macbeth* and *Bassa Moona* point the lesson of success by the pathway of originality and raciness as over against the dead hand of imitation, propaganda and the set formula.

Momodu Johnson, who later spoke disparagingly of Asadata Dafora, asserting that Dafora was not an African because an ancestor had come from Nova Scotia, laid claim to have been the chief organizer of the group

49

THE BLACK TRADITION IN AMERICAN DANCE

of African dancers. He himself led a group of dancers in July 1938 in a dance-drama, *Jungle Africa*, presented at Lewisohn Stadium.

Earlier that year a group known as the Calabar Dancers, led by Effiom Odok, had offered "A Marriage Festival in an African Village" in the sculpture court of the Brooklyn Museum. Ted Poston, writing in the *New York Post* on March 3, 1938, quotes Odok as saying that his group had been in the United States since 1921. It would appear that most, if not all, the males were African, and that the women were all Afro-American. There may well have been overlapping between Shologa Oloba, Momodu Johnson's group, and the Calabar Dancers.

In 1938 Asadata Dafora presented *Zunguru*, in the same genre as *Kykunkor*, and now called it dance-drama in deference to the preeminence of the dance. It did not have the impact of the earlier piece, and he turned his attention to the concert stage. *Zunguru* was revived in 1940, and again in 1958 with the participation of such artists as Olatunji, Esther Rolle and her sister, Rosanna Carter, who were both members of Shologa Oloba at that time.

A benefit "African Dance Festival" held in December 1943, attended by Eleanor Roosevelt and Mary MacLeod Bethune, was arranged by Dafora for the "African Academy of Arts and Research," an organization for which he was apparently responsible, having recruited Lawrence Reddick as chairman, and Alain Locke as chairman of the Education Committee. The dance critic Edwin Denby attended this program and provided an extended review of it in the *New York Herald Tribune* of December 19. Denby concluded, speaking of Dafora:

Ismay Andrews, and percussionist Chief Bey.

During 1937 the Karamu Dancers, under the direction of Margaret Witt Johnson, made their New York debut.

I think the qualities I have mentioned show him to be a remarkable choreographer as well as a fine dancer. The proportions and the sequence of the dances were excellent. But beyond this, the dancers he has trained are, after all, American girls, to whom life in an African village would be as foreign as life in a Russian one would be to the Russian-dancing Americans in our Ballets Russes. Yet this village festival (like Dafora's previous *Kykunkor* and *Zunguru*) had in performance a definite local atmosphere. It was not mere decorative exoticism. It brought with it across the ocean the sense of a real landscape and a real way of life. I wish it were possible for so sincere and intelligent a choreographer as Mr. Dafora to bring over across the ocean a small company of real West African dancers to add to his well-trained American pupils, and then show us more of the extraordinary wonders West African dancing holds.

Dafora was the organizer equally of an African-Indian-American concert in 1946 which brought together La Meri (Indian dance), Norman Coker (African drummer), Josephine Premice (Haitian folklore) and Russian-born Mura Dehn, who "interpreted" both African and modern swing rhythms. Asadata Dafora continued to experiment with the creation of African operas, two later ones being *Batanga* (1941) and *Battalokar* (1953).

Wilson Williams, 1943.

Ismay Andrews in the 1940s concentrated on dances of East Africa. Her dancers, the Swa-Hili Dance Group, performed at the Stage Door Canteen and at other venues during World War II. In December 1945, the Swa-Hili Dancers shared a program with Wilson Williams' Negro Dance Theater, of which Andrews was a member.

Black Motifs in Modern Dance

Esther Jungen, who later moved beyond the modern dance to nightclub and circus choreography, enjoyed the complete approbation of the critic John Martin, who in 1935 pronounced one of her pieces, *Animal Ritual*, to be one of the best solos done by a modern dancer. Following in the tradition of her *Go Down Death*, she included in this same recital a piece, "Negro Themes," which according to Margaret Lloyd was based on widely-published sketches of Harlem life by the Mexican painter, Miguel Covarrubias. The next year she did a piece, *Judgment Day*, apparently (like *Go Down Death*) to the reading of a sermon poem by James Weldon Johnson. Pauline Koner appeared with Jungen in this piece, which had comic elements. The same program also included "Negro Sketches" to the music of Duke Ellington.

Jane Dudley, later to be a member of the Dudley-Maslow-Bales Dance Trio, choreographed to a song by Billie Holiday in 1937 and in 1938 created *Jazz Lyric*. In 1939 Sophie Maslow did a piece called *Silcosis Blues*. In 1940 William Bales did *Black Tambourine*. After the Dudley-Maslow-Bales trio came into existence in 1942, Dudley composed a solo, *New World A-Comin'* (1945), based on the jazz idiom.

In the domain of the use of Black motifs, however, it was still Helen Tamiris who, in this period, overshadowed other dancers with her monumental composition for the Federal Theatre, *How Long, Brethren?* (1937). Presented on the same bill as Charles Weidman's *Candide, How Long, Brethren?* used a choral score based on Black protest songs. The choreography consisted of seven episodes:

I.   *Pickin' Off de Cotton*
II.   *Upon de Mountain*
III. *Railroad*
IV.   *Scottsboro*
V.   *Sistern an' Brethren*
VI.   *Let's Go to de Buryin'*
VII. *How Long, Brethren?*

The production was one of the largest-scale modern works (though it was considered a little too theatrical by some strict modernists) seen up until that time; it ran for many weeks and received general acclaim.

The creation of a modern-cum-primitive work under the auspices of the new American Ballet Theatre in 1939–40 was due to the initiative of Agnes de Mille. Hired as one of a group of choreographers for the new company, and given wide discretion as to what she might do, she opted to create a work, twenty-five minutes long, for Black women dancers; ultimately it was called *Black Ritual*. In her autobiography, *Dance to the Piper*, de Mille provides an impressionistic account of the experience:

> My company was made up of heterogeneous and for the most part untrained performers. This was before Katherine Dunham established her school, and Negroes did not train for serious dancing

because there was literally no opportunity for them to practice.

At one point I thought to change the leading dancer who, although very beautiful, failed in projection and tragic feeling. Katherine Dunham had just come on from Chicago and was waiting around for her first New York concerts. She offered her services . . . but in the end I decided to risk all on the girl I had.

The result of the experiment, according to de Mille, was disaster. The premiere performance went too slowly. And though this was corrected for the second performance, only three performances had been allotted. Critical reaction to the production was negative, and at the end of the three-week American Ballet Theatre season, the troupe of Black women dancers was disbanded. De Mille concludes:

It was good work, I think, but unlike anything else I had ever done, and jarred people. It was neither funny nor healthy, and ethnologically it was not factual. Directly Katherine Dunham came along with authentic material and everyone forgot.

De Mille was to return to the terrain of Black dance and dancers many years later as choreographer for a Broadway show, *Kwamina* (1961), which was also not a success, though the dances were praised.

Blacks on the Concert Stage

In 1931 Randolph Sawyer, who had danced with Hemsley Winfield's Bronze Ballet Plastique, joined a company created by Gluck-Sandor and Felicia Sorell, thus becoming the first Black member of a white modern dance group. In later years he appeared with Asadata Dafora, and was a member of the cast of the Broadway show *Carmen Jones*.

Add Bates became a member of the Red Dance Group, a company directed by Edith Segal. Bates frequently danced in *Black and White*, originally choreographed by Segal for herself and Black dancer Allison Burroughs in 1930. Subsequently he worked with Charles Weidman, appearing in the Weidman *Candide* (1937).

Randolph Sawyer appeared with Edna Guy as a guest artist at a concert on April 24, 1934 at Studio 61, Carnegie Hall. This concert elicited a generally favorable review from Ralph Taylor in his review for *Dance Observer*. In 1936 Edna Guy participated as a solo performer at one of the programs of the First National Dance Congress and Festival, performing on May 21, at the YMHA Auditorium.

Together with Allison Burroughs, Guy was the moving force behind the "Negro Dance Evening," held on March 7, 1937, at the YMHA. This was the occasion of the first visit of the Katherine Dunham Company of Chicago to New York. The program also included Asadata Dafora.

Guy made appearances in 1938 and in 1939, but it is uncertain whether she gave any later performances in New York. (Josephine Nicholson in her thesis was unable to document any.) Guy's dance career had extended over a decade. She is known to have worked later at a training school in New York State. She died in Fort Worth, Texas in 1983.

Around the time Guy was leaving the modern dance scene, Wilson Williams, who had studied with Helen Tamiris and Hanya Holm (and also probably with Martha Graham and Charles Weidman) began making appearances. In 1938 he appeared in an inaccurately titled "First Negro

Solo Recital of Modern Dances." In 1939, he announced the formation of a group called the Negro Dance Company which, in the course of a lecture by Williams at the Harlem YWCA, presented a "blues suite." The Humphrey-Weidman studio theater was the site of company appearances in 1941 and 1942.

Williams and the Negro Dance Company reached a new level of organization in late 1942 when they sought and obtained the attention of a number of prominent dance figures, including Anna Sokolow who was listed as giving company classes. Lecture-recitals and performances took place intermittently until December 1945, when the last recorded appearance, under the name Negro Dance Theater, took place in the Students' Dance Recital Series held at the Central High School of Needle Trades. The performing group was small, and its list of personnel completely different from that announced in 1942.

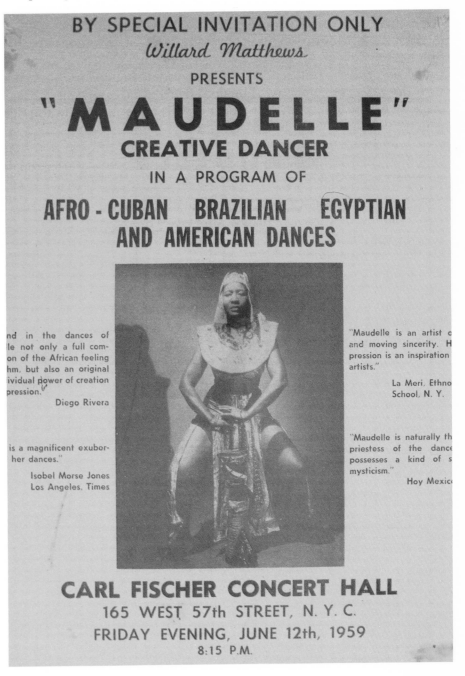

Maudelle, 1959.

In the late 1930s the dancer Maudelle worked with the Lester Horton Dance Group in Los Angeles. Maudelle, who had studied ballet, spent some time in Mexico, where she posed for the painter Diego Rivera and danced with folkloric companies. She was one of the members of Agnes de Mille's short-lived "Negro wing" of the American Ballet Theatre and performed in deMille's *Black Ritual*. Later she traveled in many parts of the world, giving dance recitals and studying various dance idioms.

In the late 1930s, also, far from the New York dance scene, Bernice Brown organized an interracial modern dance company in Minneapolis. The company performed works on Black and religious themes until its demise in 1942.

Modern Dance and the Black College

The development of American dance had been nurtured by colleges since the early 1930s; many dance pioneers held college teaching appointments, usually in departments of physical education. Institutions such as Bennington College, Connecticut College, Teacher's College of Columbia University, and the University of Wisconsin come to mind in connection with the early development of modern dance. In the 1930s two Black institutions also provided their students with opportunities in the new dance: Spelman College in Atlanta and Hampton Institute. Hampton's effort was the more massive, and its dance troupe appeared in New York and other cities. John Martin took note of the Creative Dance Group of Hampton at the time of its appearance at the YMHA in 1937:

> The group consists of forty young men and women under the direction of Charles H. Williams, supervisor of physical education, and Charlotte Moton Kennedy, instructor of physical education in the college, Hampton Institute. Both directors have been for a long time devoted students of the dance and Mr. Williams has spent a considerable portion of his time during recent Summers at the Bennington Festival and the school at Bennington College which sponsors it. It is his driving purpose to develop the rich "racial and native material" of his people along its own lines, without making race consciousness in any sense a fetish.

Frank Roberts performing the stilt dance, Mamah Parah, *Hampton Creative Dance Group, 1935.*

Writing in the *Dancing Times* of London in 1938, Michael Lorant inflated the Hampton endeavor to the status of the "Negro's Unique Dancing Academy." Invoking a rather stereotypic view of blacks, rhythm, and dancing, Lorant describes the agenda of the Creative Dance Group:

> The programme of the "Creative Dance Group" covers a wide range of subjects and offers a variety of entertainment which proves interesting not only to the lover of the dance, but to the general public as well. They dance modern, character and folk dances, including some of the American Negro of another generation, labour rhythms, spirituals, and genuine African dances, the last giving something of the tribal life and customs of the native Africans and the great abandon with which they dance.

Hampton Creative Dance Group in Wyomamie, *an African marriage custom dance, 1935, under the direction of Charles Williams, choreography by Charlotte Kennedy.*

Von Grona and the American Negro Ballet

In 1934, with some encouragement from George Gershwin and Samuel L. Rothafel (Roxy of the Roxy Theater), a German-born dancer and ballet master, Eugene Von Grona, advertised for and began to train a group of Black dancers with the intention of organizing a Black ballet company. The process of training went on for three years before a much-noticed performance at the Lafayette Theater in Harlem in November 1937 took place. The technique taught by Von Grona was derived from the Germanic tradition of Rudolf von Labon (who had taught Mary Wigman and Kurt Jooss) rather than from classical ballet.

John Martin, in doing a preview of the company in the *New York Times* (November 7, 1937), before the actual first performance, had noted:

> The materials of which the program is composed are certainly rather startling. The group itself, it seems, fell in love with the music and story of Stravinsky's ''Firebird'' when it was played for them as part of their training in music and dance background, and decided that this was to be one of their productions. They do not dance it on point, of course, or in the classic ballet technique, but adopt their own manner of telling the story. From here the repertoire goes back to Bach's ''Air for the G String'' and forward to music by W. C. Handy and Reginald Forsythe.

Critical reaction, however, including Martin's, was reserved. An unsigned review in *Newsweek* of November 29, 1937, provides an example of the responses:

(Above left) Tableau from Children of the Earth.

(Above) Children of the Earth, *choreographed by Eugene Von Grona for opening at Lafayette Theater, November 21, 1937.*

(Left) Al Bledger, ''The Body Beautiful'' soloist, Eugene Von Grona Negro Ballet, and The Von Grona Swing Ballet, 1939.

(Opposite) Lavinia Williams was a principal dancer with the Von Grona company.

Park Avenue – paying $5.50 a ticket – saw how hoofing and tapping Negroes could also perform the fanciful movements of Stravinsky's "Fire Bird." In addition the audience watching the severely formal "Religious Allegory," set to Bach's air for the G string, and two racial ballets based upon W. C. Handy's "St. Louis Blues" and Reginald Forsythe's suite, "Children of the Earth."

There were to be few additional appearances, though the troupe did have a Broadway run of nine performances in Lew Leslie's last-gasp *Blackbirds of 1939.* That show had the young Lena Horne as one of the solo singers.

Broadway Opera

Virgil Thomson's opera, *Four Saints in Three Acts* (1934), was an exciting cultural event. The music was modernist, the libretto was by Gertrude Stein, and the cast was all-Black. Using Black singers was actually an afterthought of the composer, since the subject matter, essentially surrealist, in no sense required it. The use of Black soloists, however, and of the Eva Jessye Chorus, virtually dictated the use of Black dancers for the obligatory dance elements. This was to pose something of a problem.

While the director, John Houseman, had originally proposed Agnes de Mille as the choreographer, the composer decided to use the English choreographer, Frederick Ashton, whom he had met in London the previous summer. Ashton accepted, and worked with both the singers and the dancers. Speaking of the experience, Ashton is quoted by David Vaughan as saying:

> We needed six dancers, and it was impossible at that time to find six Negro dancers who had ballet training; eventually we found three girls who'd had extremely elementary, well, *fancy* dancing . . . and we used to go to the Savoy Ballroom and pick out boys there who danced the Lindy Hop . . . and ask them if they'd like to come and do it, and eventually we got three.

While many critics noted the relative technical weaknesses of the dancers, praise for Ashton's choreographic conception was high. The next year, the production of George Gershwin's folk opera, *Porgy and Bess* (based on the 1927 Pulitzer Prize-winning play and ultimately on Du Bose Heyward's novel of 1925), was an event of great significance for Blacks in the theater. As in *The Green Pastures,* awarded the Pulitzer Prize in 1930, little formalized dancing was required in the production, but the atmospheric use of Black stance and gesture as a dramatic device was basic to the dramaturgy of the piece. This aspect of the production was usually elicited from the actors themselves, but for *Porgy and Bess* the teacher and coach Herbie Harper was hired to assist in the "dance" sequences. It may be assumed that John Bubbles, who created the role of Sportin' Life, conceived his own movement style. Subsequent productions of *Porgy and Bess* made more formal use of dance elements and of dancers, and hence of choreographers.

The work of Gilbert and Sullivan was to reach Broadway with Black casts, and some alteration in scene and setting, in two *Mikado* versions in 1939. (Subsequently *H.M.S. Pinafore* provided the substance for *Memphis Bound* in 1945.) *The Swing Mikado* was an "Africanized" production of the Chicago Federal Theater which had such an outstanding success on its

Poster for Four Saints in Three Acts, *1934.*

Bill Robinson, starring in The Hot Mikado, *1939.*

Mabel Hart, pioneer dancer, in Four Saints in Three Acts.

home ground that the idea of transferring the production to the commercial stage in New York seemed attractive as a way of increasing the budgetary resources of the Federal Theater. Mike Todd, then a Broadway producer, made overtures in this sense to the Federal Theater which rebuffed him, whereupon Todd devised the *Hot Mikado*, starring Bill Robinson, for Broadway. The Todd production was a modernized jazz one. In the end, the two productions played concurrently across the street from each other, the *Hot Mikado* clocking 85 performances, *The Swing Mikado* 86. A shortened version of the *Hot Mikado*, complete with an ad-libbing Bill Robinson, then moved to the New York World's Fair where Todd recouped his investment.

A recasting by Oscar Hammerstein of Bizet's *Carmen* led to the employment of a large number of Black dancers on Broadway in 1943. Eugene Loring was the choreographer, but he seems to have followed the practice of blocking out larger patterns and allowing the dancers to contribute details from their own movement styles. Dancers in the production included Archie Savage, Carmencita Romero, Mabel Hart, and others. Alvin Ailey and Carmen de Lavallade both danced in the much later film version of *Carmen Jones* (1954).

In 1945, Bill Robinson, then 67, starred in the not so successful *Memphis Bound*, which framed goodly chunks of *H.M.S. Pinafore* and *Trial By Jury* with a plot about Black performers marooned on a steamboat. The cast included Avon Long, the actor-dancer who had enjoyed a great success in the 1942 revival of *Porgy and Bess* as Sportin' Life.

Katherine Dunham

In 1931, the same year that the "First Negro Dance Recital in America" was presented by Hemsley Winfield and Edna Guy in New York, a dance composition "Negro Rhapsody" was presented at Beaux Arts Ball in Chicago by a group called Ballets Nègres. The group's teacher, choreographer, and chief dancer was the young Katherine Dunham. Her various roles in this enterprise were prophetic of a career which continued for over 50 years. Even the group's name, shortly to be changed to the more prosaic Negro Dance Group, foreshadowed the long involvement Katherine Dunham would have with the Black Republic of Haiti whose French-speaking milieu she was to penetrate as scholar and creator.

At the time of the Ballets Nègres performance Katherine Dunham was about 21, a student at the University of Chicago, and had been involved deeply in dance for several years. She had studied with Ludmilla Speranzeva and Mark Turbyfill. Turbyfill introduced her to Ruth Page, then dance director of the Ravinia Festival and shortly to become prima ballerina of the Chicago Opera. Page, an intrepid experimenter, had written a scenario, based on a folk tale in Lafcadio Hearne's *Two Years in the West Indies*, which was the basis for a musical score by the Black composer William Grant Still. The score, *La Guiablesse*, had been premiered at the Eastman School in Rochester, New York, with another dancer. Choreographed by Page, it was presented in Chicago in 1933, with a Black cast and Page dancing the lead. The following year it was repeated with Katherine Dunham in the role Page had created.

From the beginning, Dunham's academic interests existed in counterpoint to her interests in theatrical dance. The two were brought into closer association when she received a Rosenwald fellowship in 1935 which enabled her to undertake anthropological study of dance in the Black folk cultures of the Caribbean. Her mentors for this undertaking were Dr. Robert Redfield of the University of Chicago and Dr. Melville Herskovits of Northwestern University.

Dunham in the Caribbean
Dunham's Caribbean itinerary began in Jamaica, where she stayed in the Maroon village of Accompong, deep in the Cockpit Country, which had served as a place of settlement for escaped slaves who had been able to conserve there their African cultural elements to a greater extent than was possible in the plantation milieu. She then went to Martinique and to Trinidad for brief stays, before arriving in 1936 in Haiti. A talented writer, Dunham has chronicled her initial Caribbean experience in three books: *Journey to Accompong*, which is an anthropological journal; *The Dances of*

Katherine Dunham, 1935.

Haiti, first published in French and Spanish, an ethnographic description; and *Island Possessed*, an autobiographical account of her time in Haiti. She also wrote an extended theoretical essay on the Negro dance, part of which was published in *The Negro Caravan* (1941). In the conclusion to that selection, she wrote:

> In America, the inevitable assimilation of the Negro and his cultural traditions into American culture as such has given African tradition a place in a large cultural body which it enjoys nowhere else. While, during the cultural segregation, the African traditions were more modified here than elsewhere, those which persisted now had a sound functional relationship towards a culture which is contemporary, rather than towards one which is on the decline; and therefore such traditions as have been retained are assured of survival as long as the large, strong cultural body of which they are a part survives. With re-establishment of a functional relationship towards society as a whole (rather than to a cult) the traditions are strengthened and re-emerge with new vigor.

As a result of her research, Dunham distinguished three processes involving the African background of Black folk dance in the Western hemisphere. They are: the incorporation of African religious dance into new ritual behaviors; the secularization of African religious dance; and the interaction of African secular dance with European secular dance. Utilizing her gift for choreography, Dunham began the creation of compositions reflecting the varieties of Black folk dance she had studied. In order to train dancers to perform these works, Dunham developed a dance pedagogy based on Black dance in its Caribbean manifestation. This pedagogic vocabulary, Dunham technique, has been widely taught under many names.

Chicago and New York

On her return to Chicago, Dunham reconstituted her dance group, composing for them exercises and dances based on her Caribbean experience, particularly that in Haiti. In March 1937 she journeyed with her group to New York to take part in the Negro Dance Evening at the YMHA organized by Edna Guy.

It was at this time that she met the young dancer Archie Savage and the Haitian drummer Augustin, with both of whom she was to have an extended artistic association. In the next year she became associated with the Chicago Writers Project of the WPA. With her company, she produced the first version of her dance composition *L'Ag'Ya*, based on her research in Martinique. The designer of sets and costumes for *L'Ag'Ya*, John Pratt, became her husband the following year. He was to be associated with her work for the remainder of his life.

Near the end of 1939, Dunham returned to New York City to choreograph the 1939 version of *Pins and Needles*, a current events revue with a score by Harold Rome, which had begun its successful run as a labor union production in 1937. Dunham brought along her entire company, supporting them with her earnings, as she sought an opportunity to present her repertory to the New York public.

In 1940, the company made an emphatic entrance on the New York scene with "Tropics" and "Le Jazz Hot," at the Windsor Theater.

Tommy Gomez as Julot and Katherine Dunham as Loulouse in L'Ag'Ya, *Paris 1949.*

Cabin in the Sky

It was doubtless the impact made by Katherine Dunham and her Dancers at the Windsor which led to the entire company being engaged to appear in the all-Black musical, *Cabin in the Sky*, starring Ethel Waters. Now full-figured, Ethel Waters had been equally well known a decade before as dancer and singer. During the ensuing years, she had established herself as an all-around singer (blues, ballads, torch songs) and as a dramatic actress (*Mamba's Daughters*, based on the novel by DuBose Heyward). *Cabin in the Sky*, staged by George Balanchine, had a score by Vernon Duke. J. Rosamond Johnson was the chorus master. The play included among its choreographed segments a dream sequence, with Dunham as Cleopatra; such sequences were now identified with Balanchine's Broadway work. John Martin, writing in *The New York Times*, noted:

> . . . Balanchine has wisely allowed the dancers throughout to make use of great quantities of their own type of movements, many of them right out of the vocabulary of their own concert repertoire.

Katherine Dunham and company in Batucada, *with costumes by John Pratt, 1947.*

Frequently, however, he has forced them into his own pattern, and in the process they have lost flavor.

The "vocabulary of their own concert repertoire" was, of course, Dunham choreography.

Dancers who appeared with Dunham in *Cabin in the Sky*, among whom Martin particularly singled out Archie Savage and Carmencita Romero, included Talley Beatty, Rita Christiani, Lucille Ellis, Lawaune Kennard (Ingram), Roger Ohardieno, and Lavinia Williams. Both Williams and

The Dunham Troupe in Cabin in the Sky, *1940–41.*

Archie Savage.

Lawaune Kennard (Ingram).

Carmencita Romero.

Ingram had been in the Von Grona company. Beatty and Romero had danced with Dunham in Chicago.

After a New York run of twenty weeks, *Cabin in the Sky* went to the West Coast.

Stormy Weather
Following the closing of *Cabin in the Sky* in San Francisco, the Dunham Company made several nightclub appearances, ending in Los Angeles where an ensuing Hollywood experience had some pleasant aspects, and many unpleasant ones traceable to racism.

A Warner Brothers color film devoted to the company, *Carnival of Rhythm* (1941), was one of the best outcomes of Dunham's stay of a year in California. The best-known outcome of Dunham's California period, however, was her appearance with her dancers in the film *Stormy Weather*

(1943) where they are seen in a fog-drenched "Stormy Weather" dream sequence. The dancers in this segment, choreographed by Dunham, were Dunham herself, Talley Beatty, Janet Collins, Lenwood Morris, Tommy Gomez, Lucille Ellis, Lavinia Williams, and Syvilla Fort.

Dunham was asked, essentially as a result of the producer's confusing Tahiti with Haiti, to do choreography for *Pardon my Sarong* (1942) in which her troupe appeared, as well as the tap trio, Tip, Tap and Toe. The same year also saw them fleetingly in *Star-spangled Rhythm*, a war-time film revue.

While in Hollywood, Dunham devised a stage revue for the company, making use of pieces already composed as well as of new ones. This was to reach New York as *Tropical Revue*.

Tropical Revue and Carib Song

Tropical Revue opened in New York in September 1943, under the management of the impresario Sol Hurok, known for his work with dance companies as well as with solo artists. Hurok explains in his book, *Sol Hurok Presents,* his own motives in wandering from his accustomed Euro-classical territory.

My idea in taking over her management was to try to help her transform her concert pieces into revue material, suitable not only

Lenwood

Mor

Syvilla Fort.

to the country's concert halls, but also to the theater of Broadway and those road theaters that were becoming increasingly unoccupied because of the paucity of productions to keep them open. Certain purely theatrical elements were added, including some singers, one of them being a Cuban tenor; and, to supplement her native percussion players, a jazz group, recruited from veterans of the famous "Dixieland Band."

We called the entertainment the *Tropical Revue*. The *Tropical Revue* was an immediate success at the Martin Beck Theater in New York and, thanks to some quick work, I was able to secure additional time at the theater and to extend the run to six weeks. This set up some sort of record for an entertainment of the kind. As an entertainment form it rested somewhere between revue and recital.

Notable group pieces in this production were *Rara-Tonga*, performed by Williams, Ohardiano, Gomez, and Ellis; *Rites de Passage*; and *Plantation Dances*, which was danced by, among others, Claude Marchant and Vanoye Aikens, who were to have long and distinguished careers. Hurok's influence on the production was perceived by John Martin, who stated in his *New York Times* review (October 29, 1943):

Katherine Dunham, Tropical Revue, *1943.*

Lenwood Morris.

Formerly Miss Dunham couched the results of her intuition and study of the Negro dance in charming theatrical form always overlaid with the comment of the artist and a sense of the underlying integrity of the material. Now both that comment and that integrity appear to be sacrificed in a degree to conform to what Broadway expects the Negro dance to be. This is regrettable on two counts: first, that there are already scads of dancers who can do that sort of thing by the yard while artists of insight are comparatively rare; and second, that the material itself, which has grown out of primitive and folk research of a peculiarly sensitive kind, is not particularly suited to such treatment.

Martin's reaction to *Rites de Passage*, however, was favorable.

Roger Ohardieno and Katherine Dunham in Barrelhouse, *choreographed 1938.*

Laverne French, Katherine Dunham, Tommy Gomez in Rara Tonga, *choreographed in 1938.*

The principal new number of any length is a three-part suite called "Rites de Passage," based on primitive rituals of fertility. It is not an authentic ethnographic dance belonging to any particular locale but is an artistic creation utilizing ethnographic ideas and motives. Its movement is markedly uninhibited and certainly it is nothing to take grandma to see, but it is an excellent piece of work. Its first section, especially, is exciting and extremely well made choreographically. Possibly because there is no place left to go from here, the other two sections are slightly less effective, though in themselves they are imaginative and full of good movement. The whole work is danced magnificently by Lavinia Williams, Laverne French, Tommy Gomez, and Roger Ohardieno, with Miss Dunham in a lesser role. But it is altogether concert material, and rather inept staging and lighting do not translate it into revue.

That critics do not agree is a truism, and Virginia Mishnun, not necessarily known to fame, noted in the course of a contentious review in *The Nation* (October 9, 1943):

The most ambitious and least successful number on the program is the "Rites de Passage" based on rituals of fertility, male puberty, and death. Here, according to the program note, the attempt was made to "capture in abstraction the emotional body of any primitive community and to project this intense, even fearful personal experience, under the important change in status and the reaction of the society through this period." Although the tasteful costumes and simple, beautifully posed opening tableau set the stage for a moving performance, the superimposition of banal routines, and the failure to permit the material to determine its own form produce an opposite result.

Tropical Revue toured for two years, alienation between Dunham and Hurok increasing all the while. The reasons are made clear by Hurok:

It did not take me long to discover the public was more interested in sizzling scenery than it was in anthropology, at least in the theatre. Since the *Tropical Revue* was fairly highly budgeted, it was necessary for us, in order to attract the public, to emphasize sex over anthropology. Dunham, with a shrewd eye to publicity, oscillated between emphasis first on one and then on the other; her fingers were in everything. In addition to running the company, dancing, singing, revising, she lectured, carried on an unending correspondence by letter and by wire, entertained lavishly, and added considerably, I am sure, to the profits of the American Telephone and Telegraph Company. Columns were written about her, and fulsome essays, a good deal of which was balderdash.

During the course of the tour, Dunham and the troupe had recurrent problems with racial discrimination, leading her to a posture of militancy which was to characterize her subsequent career.

In September, 1945 Dunham brought a new dance piece to Broadway in the shape of *Carib Song*. The melodramatic storyline, the trials of a fisherman's unfaithful wife, was merely a hook upon which to hang a succession of dance sequences. Dunham's costar in the production was Avon Long. Dancers who appeared included Tommy Gomez, Vanoye

Richardena Jackson.

Gloria Mitchell.

Lucille Ellis as the Priestess, and Arthur Bell as the boy possessed, in "Shango", choreographed for Carib Song, 1945.

Aikens, Lawaune Ingram, Richardena Jackson, Gloria Mitchell, Byron Cutler, James Alexander, Eugene Robinson, Eartha Kitt, and Jesse Hawkins.

Carib Song, however, was not a commercial success, and Dunham returned to the revue format for her subsequent stage engagements.

The Trinidad Connection

While Pearl Primus – dancer, choreographer, anthropologist and teacher – was born in Trinidad, but reared and educated in the United States, several important figures on the Black American dance scene actually began their dance careers in Trinidad. They were all affected in varying degrees by a major pioneer of dance in the Caribbean, Beryl McBurnie, who was honored along with Dunham and Primus at the Twentieth Anniversary Gala of the Alvin Ailey Dance Theater in 1978.

McBurnie began her research on folkloric dance in her native Trinidad in the 1930s, after a period of doing "concert" dances with small groups of students. She had become convinced of the value of folk culture as a basis for the development of local art expressions and sought to learn more about it. In 1938, she came to New York to further her own studies in dance and pedagogy. While she studied at Columbia University and took work in modern dance, including classes with Martha Graham, she was invited to teach dances of Trinidad for the eclectic New Dance Group. During this period, she had occasion to acquaint Katherine Dunham with some of her Trinidadian material. In 1940, McBurnie returned briefly to Trinidad, where she reassembled a group and presented a varied program of dance under the title *A Trip to the Tropics*. In 1941 she was back in New York where she remained until 1945. She continued her studies and, adopting the stage name La Belle Rosette, made a number of theater and nightclub appearances. She also resumed teaching at the New Dance Group where, in 1942, the young Pearl Primus was one of her students. McBurnie presented *Antilliana*, a program of her work, at the YMHA in 1942 with a company that included Primus and Al Bledger.

In 1945 McBurnie returned to Trinidad, where she accepted the new post of dance instructor with the Department of Education. In her absence, the company she had formed had been held together and developed by the talented Bosco Holder and included among its members his brother Geoffrey. Around 1947, after an uneasy period of collaboration, Bosco Holder created his own company, and in 1948 Beryl McBurnie organized the Little Carib Theater, which served as the chief outlet for her work for many years. Bosco Holder went to England in 1950, and Geoffrey Holder succeeded him as director of the Holder Company; this disintegrated upon Geoffrey's departure for the United States in 1954. Both Holder brothers were acclaimed in Trinidad for their skill in choreography as well as in painting and design.

The Little Carib Theater included among its leading dancers Percival Borde, Kelvin Rotardier, and Molly Ahye. Both Borde and Rotardier also eventually came to the United States: the former to collaborate with Pearl Primus, who also became his wife, and the latter, following study in England, to dance with Alvin Ailey. Molly Ahye, however, remained in Trinidad and became one of its leading dance personalities. Ahye founded, directed, and choreographed the New Dance Group, which flourished from 1967 to 1975. Ahye subsequently published two books on dance in Trinidad: *Golden Heritage*, presenting a panorama of the folkloric dance, and *Cradle of Caribbean Dance*, a chronicle of Beryl McBurnie and the Little Carib Theater. Ahye also pursued graduate studies in dance in the United States at George Washington and New York Universities.

Eartha Kitt.

Bella Rosette, a stage name of Beryl McBurnie.

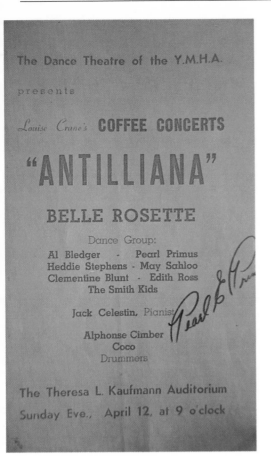

Poster for Antilliana.

Percival Borde, dancer of Trinidad.

Pearl Primus

Writing in *The New York Times* of August 8, 1943, John Martin pronounced Pearl Primus "dance debutante of the year." Primus had indeed made a spectacular debut earlier that year, exhibiting both choreographic and performing skills which marked her as an outstanding talent with a great future. Her formal involvement in dance was at that time scarcely three years old. After her graduation from Hunter College as a major in biology, her hope had been to go to medical school. In the course of odd jobs, she found herself employed in 1941 at the National Youth Administration (NYA), a federal project. There she was pressed into the dance group and immediately displayed such natural gifts that she was urged to pursue dance seriously. She enrolled in classes at the New Dance Group where such teachers as Jane Dudley, Sophie Maslow, William Bass, and Beryl McBurnie were working. Ultimately Primus studied with most of the major fountainhead figures of modern dance, including Graham, Humphrey, Weidman, Holm and Horst.

Her academic bent led her to graduate work in psychology and then in anthropology. Dance and anthropology were combined in the extended study she ultimately conducted in African dance.

Martin wrote:

Miss Primus's subjects were African, Haitian, and North American, several of the last quite naturally concerned with race oppression. What she intends her gesture to mean is always completely clear. But her sense of movement is so powerful that besides telling a story, her dance has constantly the direct force of dancing. The spring in her legs, the sweeping undulations of the torso and arms are thrilling. Her bare feet are not just feet without shoes; they can grip, caress, and strike the floor as if feeling the ground were natural to them. At several sudden high leaps the audience audibly gasped. But it is not her technique that she intends to display or that you admire, it is the dramatic form and the dramatic point of her dance. In several numbers she attains a fine Negro grandeur, and in a Haitian play dance she has a West Indian charm that is spontaneous and sweet.

From the beginning of her career as a modern dancer, Primus manifested a great interest in African themes and subjects. After her first visit to Africa in 1948, she was to devote herself almost exclusively to African dance. The reason for this specialization is perhaps expressed in a statement Primus made in 1982:

The subject matter of African dance is all-inclusive of every activity between birth and death. The seed which trembles to be born, the first breath of life, the growth, the struggle for existence, the reaching beyond the everyday into the realm of the soul, the glimpsing of the Great Divine, the ecstasy and sorrow which is life, and then the path back to the earth – this is the dance.

Pearl Primus, African Ceremonial,
1943.

Pearl Primus, Hard Times Blues, *1943.*

Pearl Primus, The Negro Speaks of
Rivers, *1943.*

Pearl Primus in Folk Dance, *1943*.

4 *Seizing the Gauntlet*

The ending of World War II initiated a general feeling of optimism about American life in which Black Americans shared. The promises of democracy which had been a necessary and inevitable part of wartime sloganeering were accepted by them as betokening a change for the better in social, economic, and political arrangements in the United States. There was much that needed to be done, even at the relatively simple level of public accommodations – Katherine Dunham's touring experiences during the closing years of the war showed that. More complex issues such as access to specialized training in various fields also awaited attention. For an intense few, one of these specialized fields was dance. Because of the nature of dance language, involving contact between the sexes both in practice rooms and in performance, Black dancers were seen by American audiences almost exclusively in segregated contexts, with the cinema making use primarily of male dancers in the relatively asexual genre of tap.

In 1946 America's best-known dance critic, John Martin of *The New York Times*, published *The Dance*, subtitled "The Story of the Dance in Pictures and Text." It was a slim book of 160 pages devoted to concert-theatrical dance, with about 60 pages on the classical ballet from its beginnings to its American manifestations, and 42 pages devoted to the modern dance, from Isadora Duncan to "Negro Dance," which was treated in three pages. In this section Martin said:

> A development that is destined to have great significance in the postwar dance world is the emergence of a number of highly gifted Negro artists. As a direct result of the old minstrel tradition, the Negro has heretofore been confined almost exclusively to the inertias of the entertainment field, but with the advent of the modern dance, in which he has found a medium for expressing himself in forms of his own devising, he has begun to find his rightful place in the creative arts and to do so with impressive results.

The list of the gifted artists which follows includes Katherine Dunham, Hemsley Winfield, the Creative Dance Group of

Pearl Primus in Dance of Strength, *1946.*

Hampton Institute, Asadata Dafora, Belle Rosette (Beryl McBurnie), Josephine Premice, and Pearl Primus. "Primus," he notes, "has exhibited magnificent gifts in the concert dance. Her technical powers are prodigious, she has temperament, imagination, and a high artistic integrity which place her at once among the best young dancers of the day, regardless of race."

Martin's book was in itself a significant event of the postwar dance scene. In 1948 the American Dance Festival was launched at Connecticut College, its founders being mindful of the legacy of the Bennington School of the Dance which had closed in 1940. The American Dance Festival (ADF) was to become a major lifeline of the modern dance and was to be hospitable to a stream of Black dance artists and students. The year before, the New York Public Library had inaugurated its Dance Collection, destined to be the preeminent research collection in its field; though for the record of Blacks in the dance, the Schomburg (another of the New York Public Library's research libraries) became the depository of choice.

In 1949, the development of serious interest in dance in the United States was marked by the publication of *The Dance Encyclopedia*, edited by Anatole Chujoy. One of its articles, "Primitive African Dance," was written by Pearl Primus; she subsequently eschewed the use of the word primitive in reference to African dance. The *Encyclopedia* included brief articles on Dunham, Primus, Bill Robinson, and Josephine Baker — and the astounded reader learned there that the last of these had studied with Balanchine!

Broadway

Most commentators are agreed that Rodgers and Hammerstein's *Oklahoma!* (1943), with choreography by Agnes de Mille, marked a major turning point for dance in the Broadway musical, the beginning of what Gerald Bordman calls "The American Musical as a Conscious Art Form." Conscious though it was, the stage *Oklahoma!*, unlike the state itself, knew no Blacks. The revival in 1946 of an earlier epochal musical, *Showboat*, however, provided an opportunity for featuring an emphatic black dance presence on Broadway in the person of Pearl Primus, already recognized as one of the outstanding figures of modern dance.

The new and renewed *Showboat* was choreographed by Helen Tamiris and included, in addition to Primus, other Black dancers such as Talley Beatty, Joe Nash, Claude Marchant, and Laverne French. It is interesting to note that the white tap-dancer Buddy Ebsen was featured in the cakewalk. The same year saw the Nicholas Brothers tapping away in the all-Black musical *St. Louis Woman*, a show which ended with a cakewalk finale. Starring Pearl Bailey, *St. Louis Woman* was based on Countee Cullen's novel *God Sends Sunday* and, despite songs by Harold Arlen, failed to create much excitement.

During this period Tamiris choreographed three other Broadway shows in which she used Black dancers: *Inside USA* (1948) (Albert

Talley Beatty.

Popwell and Talley Beatty); *Flahooley* (1951) (Joe Nash) and *Bless You All* (1958) (Joe Nash and Donald McKayle).

One of the most dazzling Broadway shows of the postwar period in terms of dance, and the one which first provided for a real integration of Black and white dancers, was the fantasy *Finian's Rainbow* (1947). The absurdist plot brings an Irish father, his daughter, and a leprechaun to the American South and subsequent hilarity as changes are rung on racial segregation. The show's choreographer, Michael Kidd, featured Black dancers such as Archie Savage, Flash Riley, and Lavinia Williams. The London production included Joe Nash and Albert Popwell.

A variety of other opportunities for Black dancers emerged on Broadway. The dancer Leo Coleman mimed the role of the gypsy boy Toby in Menotti's *The Medium* (1947); Archie Savage appeared in *South Pacific* (1949), another Rodgers and Hammerstein triumph; Ronnie Aul appeared in *Peter Pan* (1950); Jean Leon Destine and his dancers appeared in *Anna Russell's Little Show* (1953).

Among Broadway's brightest moments for the Black dancer were the Cole Porter *Out of This World* (1950), the Arlen-Capote *House of Flowers* (1954) and the Adler-Ross *Damn Yankees* (1955). Hanya Holm devised a breathtaking solo for Janet Collins as "Night" in *Out of This World*,

(Above left) Laverne French.

(Above) Claude Marchant and Jacqueline Hairston.

82

Albert Popwell.

Joe Nash.

another treatment of the Amphitryon legend. *House of Flowers*, set in an imaginary Caribbean country suspiciously like Haiti, was originally choreographed by Balanchine, who withdrew before the New York opening and was replaced by Herbert Ross. *House of Flowers* was an all-Black musical starring Pearl Bailey and Juanita Hall, among others. Its dance complement included Arthur Mitchell, Walter Nicks, Albert Popwell, Donald McKayle, Louis Johnson, and featured Geoffrey Holder in his "Banda" dance. Ross added to the cast for New York two dancers with whom he had worked in the film *Carmen Jones*: Alvin Ailey and Carmen de Lavallade.

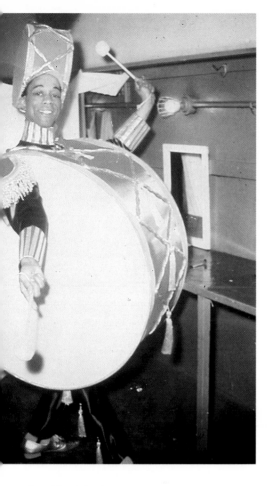

Joe Nash in Flahooley

Archie Savage.

Donald McKayle.

Damn Yankees, one of the few successful musicals ever devoted to baseball, played games with the Faust legend. Choreographed by Bob Fosse, the most spectacular dance in the musical was the baseball number performed by Louis Johnson, who repeated it in the film version of 1958.

Two operas with Black themes, in which Black dancers appeared, were produced in New York during this period, each having a limited run. *Troubled Island* (1949) by the Black composer William Grant Still, was staged at the New York City Opera by Balanchine and utilized the dancers of Jean Leon Destine. *The Barrier* (1950) with a libretto by Langston Hughes, based on his play *Mulatto*, and music by Jan Meyrovitz, was choreographed by Humphrey and Weidman and featured the Black dancer Josephine Keene.

Leo Coleman.

Louis Johnson.

(Previous pages) Walter Nicks and
Louis Johnson in House of Flowers.

''Voudou'' in House of Flowers, *Alvin
Theater, 1955.*

Finian's Rainbow, London, 1947. Dancers: Joe Nash, Dorothy McNichols, Vicki Henderson, Albert Popwell.

Geoffrey Holder.

Pearl Primus

Pearl Primus's success in *Showboat* was followed by an intermittent return to the concert stage. In the 1946–7 season she toured the college and university circuit, assisted by the dancers Joe Nash and Jacqueline Hairston. In 1948 she appeared in concert with a larger group which included Lily Peace and Matt Turney. In 1951 her assisting artists were Joe Camadore, Charles Blackwell, George Mills, and Charles Queenan, and later that same year, taking a larger group, she toured England, France, Germany and Israel.

A new Broadway opportunity seemed to emerge when she was asked in 1947 to choreograph a production called *Calypso*. The vicissitudes of this show included a name change to *Caribbean Carnival* for Broadway,

Pearl Primus, Joe Nash, Alphonse Cimber, 1946–7 concert tour.

Primus' The Initiation, *with Charles Queenan, Charles Blackwell, George Mills.*

Josephine Premice in Jamaica, *1957.*

which granted it only eleven performances. The producers had clearly expected a clone of Dunham's *Tropical Revue*, whereas Primus had a different concept. The cast included Claude Marchant and Josephine Premice, and many of the young dancers in the show had been recruited directly from the studios of the Dunham school in New York. A later Broadway experience for Primus was the play *Mister Johnson* (1956). Based on Joyce Cary's novel, the play was by Norman Rosten and starred Earl Hyman.

Expanding to Africa

In 1948 Primus received a Rosenwald grant which enabled her to make her first trip to Africa. Remaining there nine months, she had an overwhelming experience, and shared some of it with her public by way of a letter to John Martin, which he published. In Nigeria the Oni of Ife conferred on her the title Omowale – child who has returned home. Among the compositions inspired by her African experience were *Fanga*, *Prayer of Thanksgiving*, both in 1949; *Egbo Esakpade*, *The Initiation*, *Fertility*, *Hi-Life*, *Dance of the Fanti Fishermen*, all in 1950. In 1951 she assembled several of the pieces into *Excerpts from An African Journey*. In 1950, Primus appeared at the American Dance Festival, performing *The Initiation*, *Fertility*, and *Hi-Life*.

Primus undertook a research tour to her birthplace, Trinidad, in 1953 where she was welcomed by her former teacher Beryl McBurnie and where she met Percival Borde, whom she was to marry the following year. The Primus-Borde marriage ushered in a long collaboration in dance performance, teaching and research.

In the United States, Percival Borde organized a troupe of dancers which had a very successful season at the St. Mark's Playhouse in the fall of 1958, with Primus as guest artist performing solos choreographed earlier in the decade. John Martin said in a *New York Times* review (October 5, 1958):

> It is not often that dancing and music of anthropological interest are assembled with anything approaching theatrical validity, but here we are provided, however unostentatiously, with an atmosphere of simple and homely living that gives point to the ceremonial and ritual items that emerge from its background. Not every number has to be a "smash," in all conscience; some can well be made to serve more collaborative purposes. And this pleasant awareness has helped to make Mr. Borde's program both engaging and effective.

Following a second season at the St. Mark's Playhouse the following year, Primus and Borde accepted an invitation from the Government of Liberia to develop and direct an African Performing Arts Center in Monrovia. Their stay there lasted two years.

Katherine Dunham

In 1946 Katherine Dunham returned to Broadway in a revue entitled *Bal Nègre*. John Martin greeted the company in his *New York Times* review (November 17, 1946):

> In "Bal Nègre," her newest production now ensconced in the Belasco Theater for four weeks, this group finds great comfort, for here there seem to be indications of a developing rapprochement between the two hitherto apparently irreconcilable Dunhams. As in the simple performances of her early dance recital days, the breath of art is beginning to blow at least lightly down the neck of a retreating "show business." And in the healthy field of art both Dunhams should find themselves happy, unified and fulfilled. If this be wishful thinking, make the most of it.
>
> But over the show as a whole, including the many parts of it that are not new, is a new dignity, an absence of sensationalism, a new taste, that certainly interfere not at all with its values as theatre entertainment.

Percival Borde in Drums of the Caribbean, *1971.*

Katherine Dunham in Tropical Revue.

Katherine Dunham.

Katherine Dunham in Afrique.

Katherine Dunham in Cumbia.

The International Phase

Following *Bal Nègre*, Dunham returned to foreign fields: first Mexico, then Europe. The impact of Dunham's company on Europe was comparable to that which Josephine Baker had made in the 1920s. The opening of *Caribbean Rhapsody* in London in 1948 was welcomed as bringing something entirely new and necessary to the drab English postwar scene, still characterized by rationing and power shortages. The vivacity, the colorful costuming, and what was perceived as the panache of the primitive were all applauded. Richard Buckle, later to become well-known as a ballet historian and critic, produced a handsome book, *Katherine Dunham: Her Dancers, Singers, Musicians*, with photographs by Roger Wood and "other photographers." The book presents graphically what Dunham brought to England and the Continent. Buckle's introductory essay managed to be at once laudatory and patronizing:

> To some Katherine Dunham will be more interesting as a sociological than as an artistic phenomenon. It comes as a shock to learn that a Negro should successfully run the largest unsubsidized company of dancers in the United States ... that her company of magnificent dancers and musicians should have met with the success it has and that herself as explorer, thinker, inventor, organizer, and dancer should have reached so high a place in the estimation of the world, has done more than a million pamphlets could for the service of her people.

The photographic documentation of the Buckle book provides an adequate survey of the Dunham repertory seen in Europe, showing scenes from *Tropics, Son, Chorus, Nanigo, Bahiana, Shango, L'Ag'Ya, Rites de Passage, Flaming Youth,* and *Blues (Barrelhouse).*

Dancers depicted in the photographs, in addition to Dunham herself, are Lucille Ellis, Lenwood Morris, Tommy Gomez, Vanoye Aikens, Delores Harper, Richardena Jackson. Photographs of classes at the Dunham school depict the Dunham teachers Syvilla Fort and Walter Nicks, and show Eartha Kitt stretching in class. Kitt was also a member of the company during the European tour, leaving it in Paris.

The reception of Dunham and her company in Paris and elsewhere on the Continent was as enthusiastic as it had been in England, with some of the same ambiguities in perception. The critic Magdeleine Cluzel, in *Glimpses of the Theater and Dance*, provides an arresting example of this:

> Katherine Dunham enriches the theater by bringing the mystery of African rites to it, instead of letting them languish in tropical jungles. She enables us to participate today in primitive life, under immutable nature, where the visions take place in the presence of magic incantations.

The cover of Cluzel's book features a photograph of a painting of Dunham in costume by André Quellier who, according to Cluzel, had made over one hundred sketches of Dunham and the company. During the company's return engagement in Paris in 1951 at the Théâtre des Champs-Elysées (where Baker had been seen in the 1920s, and where Ailey was to appear in the 1960s), an exhibition of Quellier's Dunham studies was on view.

Dunham's European success led to considerable imitation of her work in European revues and, more lamentably, to a cultic emulation of the troupe and of its dancers, but it is safe to say that the perspectives of concert-theatrical dance in Europe were profoundly affected by the performances of the Dunham troupe which, in the course of world-wide travels in the following decade, was to become the best-known American dance company in the world, a distinction which was to be inherited by the Alvin Ailey American Dance Theater in the 1970s.

The Dunham troupe appeared in New York in 1950 before embarking on an extended tour of South America. In 1952, with her dancers, Dunham toured Europe and North Africa, in 1953 the U.S. and Mexico, in 1954 Europe again, and in 1955 South America. In the winter of 1955, the Dunham troupe returned to Broadway. A review in *Dance Observer* (January 1956) noted:

Delores Harper of the Dunham Company.

Though some of the dance content of this production seems overly theatricalized, the American Jazz section still retains much of the excitement that was apparent when Miss Dunham first brought her company to New York from Chicago in 1940. Particularly noteworthy were Katherine Dunham and Vanoye Aikens in *Barrelhouse*, the *Florida Swamp Shimmy*, and Lucille Ellis as the Kansas City woman in *Flaming Youth*.

Visually this is one of the most beautiful productions to be offered in the New York theater this year. The costumes designed by John Pratt are magnificent in their use of color, and his settings are most imaginative.

John Martin, writing in *The New York Times* (November 23, 1955), was less enthusiastic:

As a program, it is a kind of mishmash, good, bad and indifferent, in half a dozen styles, without much definition or order. Miss Dunham is the constant element. You always know exactly what she means, and it is always the same thing. Though she holds a master's degree in anthropology, it is doubtful if she could qualify for such a degree as a dancer, a singer or a choreographer. But she is a theatrical personality of full-blown and irresistible charm. Any institution would be happy to award her a Ph. D. summa cum laude.

Among the performancers who appeared in the 1955 Broadway season were Lenwood Morris, longtime ballet master of the company, Ural Wilson, Lavinia Hamilton, and Camille Yarborough. In 1956 Dunham's company extended its range to Australia, New Zealand, and the Far East. There, in Japan, in 1957, Katherine Dunham, exhausted and dispirited, dissolved the company, bringing a temporary halt to an activity in which she had been continuously engaged since the early 1930s, interrupted only by her anthropological field work of 1935–6. The overall achievement of creating and maintaining what became a major cultural institution, totally without subsidy, has few parallels in dance history. After the catharsis of writing and publishing an account of her early years, *A Touch of Innocence*, published in 1959, Dunham reconstituted the company, an experiment which was to last only three years.

Dunham's path touched the world of film at several points in her travels, and there are sequences of the troupe in the film *Casbah* (1948), and *Mambo* (1954). She choreographed for the film *Green Mansions* (1954) and *The Bible* (1964). Another activity was the commission to choreograph a new production of *Aida* at the Metropolitan Opera in New York in 1964.

The last appearance of the Dunham company in New York was in 1962, in the production *Bamboche!*, which included a contingent from the Royal Troupe of Morocco. Dunham had been absent from Broadway for seven years. Allen Hughes, who had succeeded John Martin as dance critic of the *New York Times*, wrote (October 23, 1962):

If the years have not diminished Miss Dunham's vitality, they have not made much alteration in her dance revue style either. "Bamboche!" is a hodgepodge of a show, or perhaps three shows presented under one title in one evening.

Katherine Dunham and Vanoye Aikens in Bamboche!, *1962.*

Hughes was not much pleased by the show's first part, the Moroccan section, which he found unfocussed. Of the second part, "The Diamond Thief," he says:

> The story of "The Diamond Thief," which is set in South Africa, is of no importance in itself, but it has given Miss Dunham a convenient line on which to string dances of people working, rejoicing and playing. If these dances have counterparts in South Africa, so much the better. If not, they are enjoyable all the same.

He found the third part, with its Afro-American dances, up to Dunham's par and concluded:

> "Bamboche!," then, has its bright moments if one waits for them and does not look too hard for novelty of content or treatment. In any case, Katherine Dunham is back in town, and this fact alone will probably be enough to satisfy her devoted fans.

The Dunham School

Writing in *The New York Times* (November 13, 1946), John Martin offered a capsule description of the school Katherine Dunham had established in New York in 1945:

> The Katherine Dunham School of Arts and Research is a phenomenal institution. It comprises the Dunham School of Dance and Theater, the Department of Cultural Studies and the Institute for Caribbean Research. It has two, three and five year courses leading to professional, teaching and research certificates; its faculty numbers thirty, its curriculum contains everything from dance notation through ballet, modern, and primitive techniques to psychology and philosophy, with acting, music, visual design, history and languages by the way; its student body, unaffectedly interracial, numbers approximately four hundred, and its deficits are enormous.

The description represents the ideal that Dunham had in mind, and reflects a prospectus or catalogue. In more sober fact the School was, to its students, a place to study dance. Dance being primary for most of those who enrolled, they took to culture studies with ill grace. Few were tempted by the certificate programs.

The Dunham School, located on the top floor of an unused theater on West 43rd Street, was reached by a creaky open-shaft elevator. Its classes welcomed a host of aspirant dancers, some actors, and some more or less leisured folk who sought to expand body and mind. Vitality was the keynote. The dance faculty included, from time to time, senior members of the Dunham company, but the teaching of Dunham technique ultimately came to be centered in the capable hands of Syvilla Fort, as dance director, with Walter Nicks as her assistant. These two also directed the Experimental Company, a performing group of advanced students. José Limón was among the modern dance teachers; Irene Hawthorne of the Metropolitan Opera Ballet was one of the teachers of ballet.

Though a certain number of the young male students were financed by the G.I. Bill of Rights, the overwhelming majority of the students paid little or nothing and were on "scholarship." In practice, then, the enormous deficits mentioned by Martin were chronic. Katherine Dun-

Syvilla Fort of the Dunham Company.

ham was herself the chief benefactress of the School. During the period in which the Dunham company toured constantly, virtually all of Dunham's income went into the maintenance of the School. Consequently, it is not a matter of surprise that when Dunham's income began to decline, the School was closed. By the time this occurred in 1954, the Dunham School had provided some measure of training in dance to hundreds of students.

In addition to dancers, an array of other personalities passed through the classes of the Dunham School. These included Marlon Brando, James Dean, José Ferrar, Jennifer Jones, Butterfly McQueen, Shelley Winters, and Doris Duke.

Walter Nicks in Haitian Rara Dance,
1973.

The Haitian Connection

The influence of Haiti and the folk-dances of the Haitian people on choreography and teaching in the dance world today is due chiefly to the work of Katherine Dunham. She arrived in Haiti in early 1936, after stays of varying lengths in Jamaica, Martinique, and Trinidad, all selected for study by the young dancer and aspiring anthropologist because of the depth and intensity of their African-derived dance culture. In Jamaica she had travelled to the interior, to the home of the Maroons in the Cockpit Country; her report of that experience was published as *Journey to Accompong*. Her more extended Haitian experience is recounted in *Island Possessed*. Shortly after leaving Haiti, Dunham completed a thesis on the dances of Haiti. Almost ten years later this was published as "Las Danzas de Haiti" in *Acta Anthropologica* in Mexico. A decade later, after her triumphs in France had made her well known there, a French translation was published as *Les Danses d'Haiti*, with a foreword by Claude Lévi-Strauss. Finally, *The Dances of Haiti* was published by the Center for Afro-American Studies of UCLA in 1983, but this last is a considerably revised version, incorporating a long campaign of subsequent research.

It was through her dance compositions, the Haiti-based vocabulary of movement taught as Dunham technique, and her frequent public presentations that Dunham contributed to awareness of Haiti in the world of dance and beyond. In Haiti, itself, the elite public had had very little interest in the culture of the folk, as Dunham and other commentators such as Zora Neale Hurston and Philippe Thoby-Marcelin have noted. However, in 1939 the classically-trained pianist Lina Mathon-Blanchet began to arrange Haitian folksongs for choral singing, creating groups first known as "Legba" and later as "Haiti Chante." Inevitably such a folklore group began to utilize dance as part of its programs. This process began before Dunham's work was known in Haiti, and in fact a Dunham stage production was seen in Haiti only once. However, the reputation of the Dunham Company and its broad association with Haiti developed considerable pride in, and even appreciation of, the folk dance, particularly in its sanitized theatrical versions, among Haitian opinion-makers.

The dance career of Jean Leon Destine, who was later to be the preeminent exponent of Haitian dance in the United States, began under the sponsorship of Lina Mathon-Blanchet, and was fostered by Katherine Dunham when Destine first came to the United States. Two Haitian dancer-singers who became known in the United States were Josephine Premice (actually born in the United States to Haitian parents), who herself studied at the Katherine Dunham School, and Emerante de Pradine, whose career was launched in Haiti.

In the late 1940s, as a result of its desire to make use of aspects of local culture to encourage and develop tourism, the Haitian government invited Destine to organize a National Folklore Troupe. In 1953, after the departure of Destine, the dancer Lavinia Williams was invited to Haiti to instruct members of the National Folklore Troupe and others in dance technique. This was to lead to a long association of Lavinia Williams with Haitian dance and dance in Haiti. The very next year Williams created the Haitian Institute of Folklore and Classic Dance in which she served as chief teacher, and out of which she created her own folklore troupe. Some documentation of her work is provided in her book *Haitian Dance*.

Jean Leon Destine in Festival in Haiti, *1970.*

Born in New York City, Lavinia Williams had at first studied painting at the Art Students League, but was invited to join the Negro Ballet of Eugene Von Grona. Later, when Ballet Theatre attempted to form its "Negro" wing under Agnes de Mille, she was a member of that short-lived experiment. Her studies in modern dance included work with Anna Sokolow and Martha Graham. She became a member of the Katherine Dunham Group when Dunham arrived in New York with her group from Chicago, and was a principal teacher at the Katherine Dunham School upon its opening. Later she appeared in a number of Broadway shows, notably *Showboat* and *Finian's Rainbow*. The background she took to Haiti was immensely varied and rich. The most outstanding product of her Haitian teaching career, interestingly enough, was the dancer Sara Yarborough, her daughter, who went with her to Haiti at the age of three.

Lavinia Williams later organized government-sponsored dance troupes in Guyana and in the Bahamas, and taught at New York schools including the Alvin Ailey American Dance Center, as well as at many schools in Europe, particularly in Germany.

Janet Collins and Loren Hightower in Samson and Delilah *at the Met, 1952–3.*

The African Connection

The rising tide of African nationalism, as the phrase goes, carried considerable consequences for dance in Europe and the United States. In Paris, beginning in the late 1940s, the presentations of African dance by Keita Fodeba, a philosopher teaching at the Lycée Saint-Louis, interested an avid public. In 1952, Fodeba presented a full-fledged dance company, recruited among village professionals in francophone West Africa, at the Théâtre de l'Etoile. Their success was overwhelming. Within a short time the "Ballets Africains de Keita Fodeba" had been enthusiastically welcomed in Eastern and Western Europe, the British Isles, South America, and even at home in Africa. In 1959 the Ballets Africains came to the United States to an equally clamorous reception. Fodeba explained his work in the following terms:

> In preparing our programs it has been our constant care to avoid leading the audience into error in presenting to them a picture of a fictitious Africa. It is because our songs and dances belong as much to the traditional and pre-colonial Africa of our ancestors as to the Africa of today, which little by little is becoming tinged by Western civilization. To us authenticity is synonymous with reality. To the extent that folklore is a mixture of traditions, poems, songs, dances and legends of the people, it can be no other than the reflection of the life of the country and if that country develops, there is no reason why the folklore which is the living expression, should not develop as well. That is why modern folklore in present Africa is as authentic as the Africa of old, because both are a real expression of the life of our country lived in different times of our history.

The actual production almost owed as much to Parisian stagecraft as it did to African tradition and heralded a new genre, African theatrical dance – born outside Africa, but destined to be very influential there. In due course most African nations created National Folklore Troupes, many of which have undertaken repeated tours in the tradition of the "original" Ballets Africains, whose dancers had been recruited, before decolonization, largely from present-day Senegal, Guinea, and Mali. These dancers, though villagers, were professionals, since traditional African societies held the dance in high esteem and designated talented people for intensive training in dance. The dancers in more recent African folkloric companies are likely to have had Westernized training in state schools rather than community supervision as apprentices.

The success of the Ballets Africains contributed to a widespread movement in the United States, which may be called neo-African dance. Inspired in part by ideology, but also by aesthetic impulse, African dance groups sprang up all over the United States. Many of the groups, community based, were essentially amateur and recreational; but others were fully professional. The existence of a traditional African dance tradition in New York going back to Asadata Dafora and Shologa Oloba in the early 1930s, and considerably enhanced by the work of Pearl Primus in the 1940s, provided a frame of reference for the professional companies.

On their return from Africa in 1961, Pearl Primus and Percival Borde organized an African Carnival, which was held for a weekend in November at the 69th Regiment Armory in New York. Special performers were

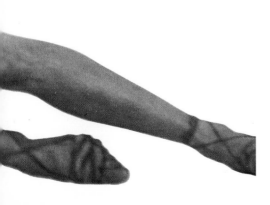

Les Ballets Africains.

Babatunde Olatunji from Nigeria, Jean Leon Destine from Haiti, Mongo Santeria from Cuba, and, naturally, Percival Borde representing Trinidad. Guests included Diahann Carroll, Johnny Nash, Cannonball Adderly and Oscar Brown, Jr. (The Nigerian Babatunde Olatunji was a master percussionist, who taught African performance traditions in his own studio, and who came to prominence in the United States when he appeared publicly throughout the country, performing and conducting classes.)

"Les Ballets Africains" returned frequently after their first visit and were followed by companies from Senegal, Mali, and elsewhere. In 1969, there was a visit by the Blue Nile Company from Ethiopia, one of the few East African companies to be seen in the United States in a field dominated by West African dance. Blue Nile developed from an ethnographic performing arts group first organized by the Egyptian-born composer Halim El-Dabh when he was a visiting professor at the University of Addis Abba, a venture regarded with suspicion by the academic authorities. It is interesting to note that El-Dabh enjoyed a close association with Martha Graham in the United States, being the composer of the score of *Clytemnestra*, as well as of *Lucifer*, the ballet that began the Graham-Nureyev association.

Neo-African Dance

Dinizulu and His African Dancers, Drummers and Singers.

One of the oldest U.S.-based African companies, known as Dinizulu and His African Dancers, Drummers and Singers, was founded by Nana Yao

Nana Yao Opare Dinizulu.

Opore Dinizulu. He began teaching African dance and culture at the Harlem YMCA in 1947, and founded his company at the same time. Dinizulu made several trips to Africa, particularly immersing himself in the African culture of Ghana, but his company, like most of the other U.S.-based companies, performs a wide spectrum of African dance.

Charles Moore, who came to African dance after extensive training in modern dance and ballet and a period in the Katherine Dunham Company, created, with his wife Ella Thompson Moore, the Charles Moore Dances and Drums of Africa. In addition to presenting indigenous dances of Africa and choreographing original dances in the vocabulary of African dance, the Charles Moore company also reconstructed dances from the repertory of Asadata Dafora and Katherine Dunham.

The Chuck Davis Dance Company, based in the Bronx, attracted a large public to their performances of African dance, even carrying their performances of Yoruba dance ritual to Nigeria during FESTAC, the international festival held there in 1977. The Bronx company was later dissolved by Davis, who created a new community-based company in North Carolina, which has often been a resident company at the American Dance Festival in Durham.

Charles and Ella Thompson Moore in Souvenir d'Haiti, *1976.*

Charles Moore in Sacred Forest.

Chuck Davis' African American Dance Ensemble, 1988.

In 1958, Arthur Hall founded the Afro-American Dance Ensemble in Philadelphia. Though not exclusively devoted to African dance, the company has become known primarily for its African repertory and frequently does programs consisting entirely of African dance. In 1969 Hall opened a community center in which teaching of African dance is integrated with other subjects. Now known as the Ile Ife Center for the Arts and Humanities, it includes a museum and a theater. Another outstanding community company is that founded by Melvin Deal in Washington, D.C., which has been an important part of the artistic fabric of that city.

Chuck Davis and others initiated "Dance Africa," a festival of African American dance companies, at the Brooklyn Academy of Music, which became an annual event. The 1979 program presented the following companies:

Dinizulu and His African Dancers, Drummers and Singers
Chuck Davis Dance Company
Charles Moore and Dances and Drums of Africa
The International Afrikan American Ballet
The Little Black Heritage Dancers

111

By 1985, the three-night celebration presented the following array of companies:

Arthur Hall's Afro-American Dance Ensemble
A Touch of Folklore and More
Calabash Dance Theater
Charles Moore Dance Theater
Chuck Davis Dance Company
Dinizulu and His African Dancers, Drummers and Singers
International Afrikan American Ballet
Izulu Dance Theater (Isizwe)
Muntu Dance Theater
Ko-Thi Dance Company
Sabar Ak Ru Afriq
The Art of Black Dance and Music
The Bernice Johnson Dance Company
Women of the Calabash

By and large, the dancers in the neo-African companies perform for the sheer love of dance and do not expect to earn even the precarious living which most professional dancers hope to gain from their art. The audiences for the companies are drawn from a wide spectrum, but include many people who do not often see other varieties of concert-theatrical dance. There is, consequently, an uneasy overlap of neo-African dance and other dance forms, leading to tensions with critics, funding sources, and presenters. The vitality of neo-African dance, however, has been reaffirmed continually since the 1960s.

Modern Dance/Black Dancers

Modern dance, from its very origins ideologically attuned to the idea of a democratic America, inspired by the artistic spirit of Whitman and Emerson, and giving primacy to American and colloquial themes, has been relatively hospitable to the Black dancer. For practical, rather than aesthetic, reasons early modern dance companies consisted chiefly or exclusively of women dancers, though the earliest Black dancers to appear in integrated companies were men.

By the 1940s, a number of Black dancers, male and female, had trained in the studios of the major modern dance pioneers and their disciples, and the appearance of Pearl Primus on the modern dance scene in 1943 may be said to have placed the Black dancer in the mainstream of modern dance. Primus was at first primarily a solo dancer, choreographing dances suited to her special gifts, and her subsequent development was centered on research in and theatrical presentation of African and Afro-Caribbean dance.

A male dancer of great promise emerged on the modern dance scene in the early 1950s in the person of Ronnie Aul, a dancer with the Dudley-Maslow-Bales Company. Of him, at his 1952 ADF appearance, critic Walter Terry said:

> Here is a dancer with a body-instrument trained to obey every command. He can move with incredible swiftness. . . . He can leap, jump, fall, twist or turn with the utmost ease.

At ADF in 1953 Aul presented two solos, *Sonata for Dancer and Piano* and *30th at 3rd*. His Broadway appearances included dance or mime roles in

Arthur Hall in Obatala Festival, *1970.*

Peter Pan (1950) and *Camino Real* (1953). Though he had presented a New York recital in 1952, he subsequently went abroad, teaching and dancing in Europe and then in Martinique.

Ronnie Aul.

The 1950s saw the entrance of two Black women into the Martha Graham company. Mary Hinkson was to become a quintessential Graham dancer, inheriting in later years many of Graham's own roles. After studies in ballet in Philadelphia, Hinkson majored in dance at the University of Wisconsin where Matt Turney, whose career was to parallel hers, was a classmate. The two came to New York in 1951 to study at the Graham School, and the next year were invited to join the company.

Hinkson danced with John Butler and Pearl Lang, studied dance composition with Louis Horst, and ballet with Karel Shook. While her principal activity was with the Graham Company, she made significant guest appearances. In 1961 she danced in Balanchine's *Figure in the Carpet*, with the New York City Ballet; in 1964 she appeared in John

Mary Hinkson in Part Real – Part Dream, *1967.*

Butler's *Carmina Burana*, with the New York City Opera (Carmen de Lavallade was also in the cast), and in 1966 in Glen Tetley's *Ricercare* with the American Ballet Theatre.

The Martha Graham company also welcomed such dancers as Clive Thompson, Dudley Williams, and William Louther, all of whom are also noted for their affiliation with the Alvin Ailey company, though Louther's stay with Ailey was brief.

The José Limón Company included a number of Black dancers, notably Clay Taliaferro, John Parks, and Clyde Morgan.

While many other Black dancers, such as Donald McKayle and Gus Solomons who have achieved great prominence as choreographers and company directors, have appeared with major modern companies, the Black presence in the modern dance has not been unproblematic. Some directors and choreographers have felt that often Black dancers, even given a role which was not race-specific, were ''inappropriate.'' The

Clive Thompson.

occasional perplexity of a critic may be illustrated by Arlene Croce's discussion of Paul Taylor's *American Genesis*, which she found a pleasant piece, but at times confusing. In *The New Yorker* of April 1, 1974, she wrote:

> And sometimes the casting sets up problems of its own. Taylor apparently couldn't resist following the Plymouth Rock scene with a Colonial-era minuet to a Haydn quartet, in which Lilith is introduced to Adam. But we have no way of knowing (unless we've read the program) that Carolyn Adams is Lilith or Greg Reynolds Adam, and because they are both black dancers we may think at first that they're supposed to be slaves. When we consult the program to find out who the other two (white) dancers in the minuet are, we read "Other Adam and Lilith," which simply won't do. Taylor doesn't use his black dancers for their blackness, and he seems deliberately to have avoided turning the Cain-Abel story into the Civil War. Yet the logic of the scenario is such that we expect certain explicit encounters and events to occur; we're compelled to seek links in the action where Taylor provides none.

116

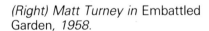
William Louther in Hermit Songs, *1978.*

(Right) Matt Turney in Embattled Garden, *1958.*

Carolyn Adams was considered by Croce and others to be one of the best dancers in the Paul Taylor company, where she was to spend her entire performing career.

Blacks and Ballet

Writing in *Ballet News* (March 1983), Clive Barnes, the English-born dance and drama critic observed "... the position of the black classic dancer in American ballet has never been strictly kosher," and he asked, "Where indeed *is* the black classic dancer?" He lists quite a few: Arthur Mitchell, John Jones, Christian Holder, Christopher Boatwright, Kevin Pugh, Billy Wilson, Sylvester Campbell, Paul Russell, Keith Lee. Barnes notes that (except for Mitchell, Jones, Holder, and Lee) they had had to find places abroad in Germany, the Netherlands, Scotland, and Canada. Barnes contrasted ballet with some other art forms:

> Opera organizations have had no such difficulty in assimilation, and the theatre has also done reasonably well. Films and television are quite obviously color-blind. Why does classic dance persist in lagging behind?

While he perhaps overstated the case of racial harmony in the other areas, it was the ballet which was under scrutiny. He then rehearses the two reasons offered most frequently for the state of affairs:

> It has, naturally, been suggested that the black physique, while suitable for modern dance, is not ideal for classic ballet. This is balderdash – it reminds me of the suggestion once made to Edwin Denby that Nijinsky went so high in the air because the bones in his feet skeletally resembled a bird's. But birds don't fly with their feet, Denby replied. Anatomically, there seems to be no basic difference between blacks and whites.

> What perhaps is more to the point is that the lack of expectations of success in classic dance has meant in the past that blacks started classes later and were more prepared to make their careers in related fields than their white colleagues. Yet since the pioneer teaching work of the Dance Theatre of Harlem, and, more recently, the Eliot Feld School, which buses minority students in for classes, even this won't quite wash.

The occasion for Barnes's article having been the entry of Mel Tomlinson into the New York City Ballet, he concluded on a jaunty note:

> In fairness, Mikhail Baryshnikov's use of Perry at ABT does seem more openminded than the deal black dancers have been given in the past. So perhaps one day, we will see more black faces in the audience as well as on the stage, and black will be proven beautiful in ballet as well as in life. Meanwhile, welcome, Mel Tomlinson – and remember, kid, this is a free country. You don't have to try any harder than Peter Martins.

In fact, this was not the first foray made by Barnes on this topic in the world of ballet. In 1971, a few years after the creation of the Dance Theatre of Harlem, there was a gala performance at the New York State Theater in which the company was featured along with the New York City Ballet. There was some criticism that while NYCB dancers did the more "classic" portions of the work especially choreographed by Balanchine and Mitchell for the occasion, the DTH (read Black) dancers did the more "ethnic" portions. Barnes said on this occasion that there should be more integration in the NYC Ballet. This inspired a spirited, if sprawling and incoherent, response from George Balanchine, as reported in John Gruen's *The Private World of Ballet*:

> He says he would like to see more black faces in the company. Well, I can answer that. I would like to see a lot of black people writing his articles. Why not? Are they so bad? Can't they write ballet criticism? As you know, I started as a choreographer many years ago. And many years ago, I wanted to have very-well-trained black people dancing. You must understand that Negro blood or Japanese blood or Russian blood doesn't mean a thing to me. I don't take people because they are black or white. I take exquisite people – people who are made to dance certain types of dancing, which for me is mainly classical dancing. You have to have a certain kind of build, because otherwise you will suffer. The fact is, we have black children in our school. But they don't stay in the school long enough. It's always like that, with whites and blacks. Mothers

John Jones in Gamelan, *1967.*

Stephanie Dabney in Firebird, *1983.*

Keith Lee.

would come to me and ask how long it will take her child of eight to become a ballerina. I say it takes about eight to ten years. Then it takes another ten years. So, it's about twenty years' work, and that, of course, only if God blesses these ballerinas to really become first class. Well, the mothers say, "Oh, no, that's too long." Then they take their children away.

After a brief digression, Balanchine continued, revealing perhaps more than he knew:

When I took Arthur [Mitchell] there were many objections. People said, "What are you going to do with him? He is black." I said, "He will dance." Finally, he became integrated, not in a black sense but in a whole sense. He danced for many years in the corps. Then I started to give him other things to do. I don't want to see two Japanese girls in my *Swan Lake*. It's not right. It's not done for them. It's like making an American blonde into a geisha. It's a question of certain arts being things unto themselves. Japanese art is one thing; Chinese art is another. You cannot change what's inherent in a particular art form. As for my critics, these people . . . it's not their business to dictate to other people. They can say when a ballet is terrible, they can say that a dancer is no good, but they cannot tell me what I should do.

It should be noted that *Swan Lake* is done in Japan by Japanese dancers. On the other hand, on the one occasion when this writer met Léonide Massine at a party in Paris in 1958, that great Russian choreographer expressed confusion as to why Japanese should dance classic dance when their "own things" were so refined.

Beyond the question of the level of technique and sense of application demanded of the classical dance, there are clearly "liminal" and subliminal factors which enter into the question of the use of Blacks in classical dance. For earlier American audiences the mere act of touching between members of the opposite sexes of different races was a gross breach of propriety. For later audiences the implied eroticism of interaction between male and female audiences in ballet invokes deeply felt taboos against interracial sex, just as male coupling in the work of Béjart has evoked the taboo against homosexuality, accounting in part for the virulent critical response Béjart receives in the United States.

Beyond "liminal" factors which white choreographers and ballet masters might not be expected to share with audiences and critics, there is perhaps a subliminal one based on a notion of color harmony which, particularly in large ensemble dancing, seems implicit in the idea of "white" ballet, despite the supposed reference of that term to costume rather than skin tone.

Pioneers and Teachers

One of the first American Blacks to receive training in classical ballet was Helena Justa-De Arms. Born in 1900, she went at the age of four with her vaudevillian parents Mae Wells and Duke Johnson to Europe, where they remained for six years. She was promptly enrolled in a ballet academy in Brussels, and soon became an adjunct to her parents' act as the "dancing baby." After her return to the United States around 1910, Justa-De Arms spent a number of years in school and at the age of 17 returned to vaudeville, doing chiefly ballet routines. She later appeared in such shows as Lew Leslie's *Blackbirds*, where ballet was not required.

By the 1930s, however, several Blacks had managed to "bootleg" training with the various Russian and other emigre ballet teachers who had begun settling in the United States in the 1920s. Not yet sharing the prejudices of "established" emigrants, they often consented to teach Blacks privately or in small separate classes. From this group emerged exceptional teachers. It should be noted that Katherine Dunham's studies in Chicago with Ludmilla Speranzeva were in classical ballet, and it was classical ballet which Dunham taught to her first students and used as the basis of her first "Black" dances.

In Boston, Doris Jones studied ballet with Lula Philbrook and then taught ballet to her own pupils. Jones later moved to Washington, D.C., where she opened the Jones-Haywood School in partnership with Claire Haywood in 1940. One of Jones's outstanding pupils in Boston was Elma Lewis, who became a teacher at the Jones studio in Boston. Following Jones's departure, Lewis opened her own school which eventually became the Elma Lewis School of Arts and the nucleus for the National Center of Afro-American Artists. Lewis has had an important impact on the dance and the development of the Black dancer, a fact which gets lost

Arthur Mitchell and Suzanne Farrell in George Balanchine's Agon, *1957.*

in the welter of her other achievements in arts and community organization.

Doris Jones and her partner Claire Haywood developed a highly regarded school in Washington, and when the Ford Foundation funded a national dance teaching project under Balanchine's direction, they were included as exemplary teachers. In 1961 Jones and Haywood created the Capitol Ballet; this presented a succession of creditable performances in which Jones's considerable skills as a choreographer were revealed. The May 1966 performance, which included *Epigrams*, a ballet by Arthur Mitchell, offered three pieces by Jones: *Ebony Concerto* to Stravinsky's score, *Bach Variations*, and *Pocahontas* to a score by Elliot Carter originally composed in 1937 on commission by Lincoln Kirstein for Ballet Caravan. Other ballets by Jones for the Capitol Ballet were *The Stephen Foster Suite*, *Italian Symphony* (Mendelssohn) and *Flair for Movement* (Gustav Holst). The roster of dancers who studied at the Jones-Haywood school includes Louis Johnson, Sylvester Campbell, Chita Rivera, Hinton Battle, Sandra Fortune and Renee Robinson.

In Philadelphia from 1934 until the period of World War II, a remarkable enterprise in the teaching of dance (chiefly ballet) was conducted by Essie Marie Dorsey. Dorsey had studied with both Fokine and Mordkin and, during her study with the latter, was able to help a young dancer, William Dollar; he went on to achieve much success as dancer and choreographer, and subsequently provided training opportunities for some of her students. Dorsey's original teaching in Philadelphia had been in the 1920s. She moved to Baltimore where she also had a studio, returning to Philadelphia in 1934. Her own study extended to Spanish dance and other styles, all of which she taught with enthusiasm and vigor. Several of her students became the leading teachers of Black dancers in Philadelphia in the 1940s and later. These included Marion Durham Cuyjet, John Hines, and Sidney Gibson King. Dorsey also taught Mary Hinkson, later of the Graham Company, and Joan Myers, director of the outstanding regional company, Phildanco.

King and Cuyjet were at first assistants to Essie Marie Dorsey and after Dorsey's temporary retirement (Dorsey was to return to active teaching in the late 1940s), they opened a joint studio. Subsequently, they each opened a school. The Judimar School was created by Cuyjet in 1948. Judimar employed outstanding teachers, some of whom commuted regularly from New York. Among these were Walter Nicks, Joe Nash, and Ernest Parham. Essie Marie Dorsey herself taught Spanish dance, and later ballet for Judimar. Among the outstanding students of Judimar, all of whom concentrated on ballet, were: Delores Brown, John Jones, Frances Jiminez, Billy Wilson, Tamara Guillebeaux, Donna Lowe, China (Melva) White, and Judith Jamison.

In New York City Mary Bruce conducted an extensive dance program at her school in Harlem, beginning in 1938, following a decade of teaching in Chicago. Her annual "starbuds" recitals, frequently held at Carnegie Hall, introduced the idea of concert-theatrical dance to many Black New Yorkers.

Ballet Companies

Inspired – rather than daunted – by the difficulty of access to the large ballet companies, a number of Blacks in the post-World War II era made efforts to form all-Black classical ballet companies. These efforts all

Sylvester Campbell and Yoko Ichino in Le Corsaire, *Bolshoi Theater, 1977.*

Sylvester Campbell in Jack Carter's Pas de Deux Romantique, *1973.*

shared, in an exaggerated manner, the hazards and perils attendant upon the creation of small and provincial ballet companies in the United States: underfunding, inadequate training, limited audience support. An analogy might be made with opera, another area in which several all-Black efforts were made in response to exclusion from larger opera stages. Opera ventures, however, have been more successful.

Leaving apart fugitive and "program" companies which were simply periodic student recitals, we may note the Hollywood Negro Ballet, founded in 1949 by Joseph Rickard. There was a highly experimental attempt of Aubrey Hitchins to form an all-male Black ballet company under the name of the Negro Dance Theater in 1956. The company appeared at the Jacob's Pillow Festival that year.

The most considerable attempt at the formation of all-Black ballet, however, was that of Ward Flemyng, whose company Les Ballets Nègres, created in 1955, was known in 1957 as the New York Negro Ballet and ultimately, at a 1958 YMHA concert, as Ballet Americana. The company did a brief European tour in the fall and winter of 1957. Closely associated with the company as dancer, and then codirector, was Thelma Hill, later to achieve eminence as a teacher. Other dancers associated with the company were Delores Brown and Frances Jiminez, both products of the Judimar School in Philadelphia, and Sylvester Campbell, a product of the Jones-Haywood School in Washington, D.C.

The 1958 concert of Ballet Americana included among its dancers Eugene Sagan, Guy Allison, Cleo Quitman, Elizabeth Thompson, Anthony Basse, Robert Tadlock, and James Thurston. Choreography was by Louis Johnson, Audrey Basse, and Ernest Parham.

In Washington, D.C., the Capitol Ballet, based on the Jones-Haywood School, gave impressive programs from 1961 to 1978, utilizing well-trained pupils of the school and guest artists, both white and Black. In Boston, the National Center of Afro-American Artists organized a dance company, at one time directed by Talley Beatty, which in 1971 (and later under Billy Wilson) included ballet works in its repertory.

Black Dancers in ''White'' Ballet

By the 1940s, it was clear that classical ballet was to be at home in the United States, and a certain rapprochement in teaching and performing began to develop between the ''foreigner'' and the home-grown dance. Ballet Theatre, later American Ballet Theatre, had issued from the shell of the Mordkin Ballet in 1939. The Ballet Russe de Monte Carlo, with its Russian and Russianized dancers, had been touring the length and breadth of the land since 1938. And in 1946 Lincoln Kirstein and George Balanchine created Ballet Society, which continued the work they had been doing with their American Ballet Caravan until 1941, and laid the foundation for the New York City Ballet (NYCB) which was to come to life in 1948.

Only the brief episode of Agnes de Mille's all-Black female less-than-

Joseph Rickard's Hollywood Negro Ballet, 1949.

Joseph Rickard's Harlot House *with Thelma Hill, Edinburgh Festival, 1957.*

Ward Flemyng.

Bernard Johnson, choreographer, lead dancer with Ballet Americana.

Delores Brown, soloist, Ballet Americana.

classical wing of Ballet Theatre had saved America's ballet companies in the early 1940s from being lily-white through and through. In 1947 the new Ballet Society cast Talley Beatty in its production of Lew Christiansen's *Blackface*, but other discussed Ballet Society projects in which Beatty might have been used never materialized. In the next decade, however, the example of modern dance and, one might suppose, the imperatives of democracy in the arts, brought a few well-trained Black dancers to the stages of the ballet establishment.

At the opening of the 1951–2 season, Janet Collins made her debut as prima ballerina of the Metropolitan Opera House in Margaret Webster's restaging of *Aida*. Collins had created a sensation dancing the choreography of Hanya Holm in Cole Porter's *Out of This World*, and was in fact an excellent modern dancer. But her primary interest was in ballet, and in Los Angeles she had studied ballet from childhood on, including lessons with Carmelita Maracci, Mia Slavenska and Adolph Bolm. She had once auditioned for Léonide Massine and the De Basil Ballet Russe Company. According to Margaret Lloyd, "He was very kind and found nothing wanting in her technique but, he said, to use her he would have to create special parts for her, or paint her face white."

On the West Coast Collins danced with Lester Horton and briefly with Katherine Dunham. She also devoted herself to choreography, for which she received a Rosenwald grant (joining Dunham and Primus in that distinction). Coming to New York in 1948, she drew accolades after a debut recital at the YMHA. *Out of This World* followed, and ultimately, ballet at the Metropolitan. Collins toured extensively as a solo dancer in her own choreography which included versions of the spirituals, as well as pieces such as *La Creole* and *Après le Mardi Gras*, reminiscent of her birthplace, New Orleans. Her work in ballet, however, was limited to the opera stage.

In 1952, Jerome Robbins selected Louis Johnson to appear in his NYCB ballet *Ballade*, but Johnson did not enter the company. However, in 1956 NYCB added Arthur Mitchell to its roster. Mitchell's first distinctive role was in a ballet by the modern dance choreographer, John Butler, to a score by Gian-Carlo Menotti. Originally commissioned by the Coolidge Foundation at the Library of Congress, the ballet, *The Unicorn, The Gorgon, and the Manticore*, was premiered in Washington, D.C. in 1954 with Talley Beatty in the role of the Unicorn. The NYCB production presented Mitchell in that role in January 1957.

In the fall of 1957, Mitchell created what was to be one of two signature roles in a long and distinguished career at NYCB, that in Balanchine's *Agon*. Several seasons later in 1962, his dancing of the role of Puck in Balanchine's *A Midsummer Night's Dream* was also widely applauded.

Reporting on Mitchell's performance in *Agon* in Moscow in October 1962, Lincoln Kirstein (in his *Thirty Years*) reveals that Soviet aesthetes had some of the same difficulties with the piece that Arlene Croce had experienced with regard to Paul Taylor's *American Genesis*:

> In *Agon*, for example, Arthur Mitchell, our elegant black soloist, performed the crucial *pas de deux*, cold as spring water in its dispassionately erotic acrobatics. . . . In the *Agon pas de deux* Balanchine had arranged one of his most ingenious serpentine, linked patterns in equal balance between partners of opposite sexes. In certain passages Mitchell's pantherine sinuosity tended to swing the combination into approximately a star turn. In the Muscovite press, however, Balanchine's expression of Stravinsky's mutations of Mersenne and de Lauze's Renaissance dances was interpreted as a Negro slave's submission to the tyranny of an ardent white mistress. Andrei Balachivadze, in conversation, at least, expressed admiration for his brother's tact, daring, and taste in presenting a white girl and black boy in such an implicit and prolonged design. This element has caused no comment at home in the five years of its existence.

Mitchell was to have a distinguished role as soloist with NYCB before reducing, then terminating his activity in the company as he shaped the Dance Theatre of Harlem. In 1960, he danced in Balanchine's *The Figure in The Carpet* in which Mary Hinkson, appearing as a guest artist, was his partner. In the same year, in the collaborative "Jazz Concert," he appeared in Todd Bolender's *Creation of the World* and John Taras's *Ebony Concerto*. Mitchell also went on to create roles in two other ballets by Taras (*Arcade* in 1963 and *Piège de Lumière* in 1964) and at least six by Balanchine (*Clarinade* in 1964, *Don Quixote* (Mitchell in Flamenco) in

Raven Wilkinson in "Valse" from Les Sylphides, *Ballet Russe de Monte Carlo, 1960.*

Janet Collins at the Met in Aida, *1952.*

Christopher Boatwright and Amelia Holst, LINES Dance Company, 1987.

1965, *Divertimento No. 15 (II)* in 1966, *Trois Valses Romantique* in 1967, *Metastaseis and Pithoprakta*, and *Slaughter on Tenth Avenue*, both in 1968).

In 1961, Balanchine choreographed a ballet, *Modern Jazz Variants*, to a score by Günther Schuller, using both an orchestra in the pit and the Modern Jazz Quartet on stage. The dancers were the ballerinas Diana Adams and Melissa Hayden, and Arthur Mitchell, all company members, and John Jones, appearing as guest artist. After his studies in ballet at the Judimar School, Jones had studied with Anthony Tudor and Margaret Crask at the Metropolitan Opera Ballet School, and then at the School of American Ballet with Stanley Williams.

By the time of his guest appearance with NYCB, Jones had danced with the Katherine Dunham Company and with Jerome Robbins' Ballets: U.S.A. In subsequent years he appeared with the Joffrey Ballet, the Harkness Ballet, the Dance Theatre of Harlem, Arthur Hall's Afro-American Dance Company, the American Dance Machine, and the Rod Rodgers Company.

Among the many Black ballet dancers who danced in companies abroad during the 1950s and later was Delores Brown, a fellow student of Jones at Judimar, who appeared in Cuba with Alicia Alonso's Ballet Alonso. Brown later joined the company of the National Center for Afro-American Artists in Boston, and then had a distinguished career as ballet teacher at the Alvin Ailey School and as company teacher for the Ailey company.

5 *Decades of Achievement*

Talley Beatty's Tropicana, *1950–55.*

Gary DeLoatch in Talley Beatty's The Stack Up, *1983.*

The mid and late 1950s mark the beginning of the wide-scale participation of Black dancers and choreographers in American concert-theatrical dance, paralleling the dramatic expansion of dance as an autonomous and respected art form on the American scene. While constraints continue to operate, attributable largely to racist institutions and attitudes, the manifestation of Black talent after fairly open access to training, the impact of the Civil Rights Movement of the 1960s, and the virtual explosion of Black creative and organizational talent in the 1970s, all assure a strong and obvious Black presence in American dance in the last third of the century.

The leading choreographers who had emerged by 1960 were Alvin Ailey, Talley Beatty, Donald McKayle, and Louis Johnson. Hard upon their heels came Eleo Pomare, Gus Solomons, Jr., and Rod Rodgers. In the next two decades the ranks expanded to include Garth Fagan, Diane McIntyre, Bill T. Jones, Ulysses Dove, and a host of others. Most of the choreographers began as outstanding dancers and their respective companies and works revealed to the dance world a thrilling assemblage of brilliant and accomplished dancers.

While Broadway declined as an outlet for dancers and choreographers, except for a few outstanding exceptions, off-Broadway activity and regional theater provided some opportunity for "movement" staging. The flourishing of pop singing groups and their employment of choreographed routines provided some outlet for choreographic talents, and the music video genre of the 1980s provided outlets both for choreographers and dancers. Television film and, to a lesser extent, general release films, opened up dance vistas, including an anemic revival of tap.

The major streams of American concert-theatrical dance underwent contrasting experiences during this period. When the New York City Ballet was given a permanent base at the New York State Theater in Lincoln Center in 1964, its geographical proximity to the Metropolitan Opera and the New York Philharmonic seemed to pronounce the reception of American ballet into a rarified establishment. On the other hand, around

1962, American modern dance was subjected to a searching examination and apparent rejection by a younger generation in a movement to which the terms "post-modern" and "minimalist" have been applied, and which was also known by the name of one of its major venues, Judson. The Judson Dance Theater, located at the Judson Church in Greenwich Village, became the outlet for dancers anxious to abandon what they regarded as "slickness" in conventional modern dance. For many of the rebels, a basic need was to expunge "reference" in their compositions. Many of the white dancer-choreographers associated with this new movement, such as Lucinda Childs and Twyla Tharpe, have subsequently become "slick" and highly referential.

Black choreographers and dancers were not conspicuous in the "post-modern" movement since, responding to the weight of social concerns which oppressed them as individuals, they still found much to explore and assert in the older traditions of message or content modern dance. A notable exception to this generalization was Gus Solomons, Jr. who not only pursued movement as movement, but who resisted the later pull towards "slickness" and assimilation to the establishment felt by many of his white colleagues.

Dancers and Critics

During the 1960s the question of the relation of critics and criticism to arts and artists of Black America was increasingly discussed. In part, this was a reflection of the socio-political climate in which Black grievances concerning discrimination and oppression were being articulated with greater frequency and intensity. In one sense these discussions evoked similar discussions during the Harlem Renaissance and the 1930s. However, the use of the term "Black aesthetic" in the 1960s spoke of a new sense of urgency, if not of rigor. As Carolyn Fowler states in the Introduction to her *Black Arts and Black Aesthetics*:

> ... the black aesthetic school for the first time articulated philosophical implications by bringing a terminology to the tradition. They staunchly maintained that a specific world view, an ethos, a sensitivity exist in the black community, and have resulted in a specific creative tradition, both in the arts and in everyday life.

Whether or not specific Black dancers and choreographers were persuaded by or even particularly aware of, the elaboration of Black aesthetic theory, many felt that they were the victims of misunderstanding and consequent undervaluing by influential members of a white critical establishment. The June 1973 issue of the short-lived Black dance monthly *The Feet* conducted a forum, "Black Choreographers and Dancers Speak on the Value of Critics." Questions were addressed to Arthur Mitchell, Rod Rodgers, Eleo Pomare, Carmen de Lavallade, Raymond Sawyer, Donald McKayle, and Claire Haywood of the Jones-Haywood School in Washington, D.C.

Four of the questions were:.

There followed a number of other experiences, including study at the School of American Ballet, and appearing in an experimental Maya Deren film, *A Study in Choreography for the Camera* (1945), in which the film follows Beatty in the process of creating a dance composition. Talley Beatty's enormous technical skills as a dancer were deployed in several Broadway shows, notably *Showboat* (1946) and *Inside USA* (1948). During this period he also taught at the Katherine Dunham School. In the 1950s, Talley Beatty organized a dance company which toured the college and recital circuit in a program entitled *Tropicana*. *Tropicana* followed the format of many of the Dunham productions, offering a medley of Afro-Caribbean and Afro-American dance solos and group pieces, interspersed by drum and vocal interludes.

One of the most appreciated pieces in the Beatty program for several years was *Southern Landscape*, whose program notes were as follows:

"When the eight years Reconstruction period of Negro and White freedom and cooperation in the South was destroyed, it was destroyed completely."

a.   THE DEFEAT IN THE FIELDS
     While working in their fields, the people are terrorized by the newly formed Ku Klux Klan. The men go off to fight and return defeated.

b.   MOURNER'S BENCH

c.   MY HAIR WAS WET WITH THE MIDNIGHT DEW
     Under emotional stress the survivors wandered at night through their ravaged fields.

d.   RING-SHOUT
     The defeated seek release through the ring-shout (a survival of an African religious dance)

e.   SETTIN' UP
     The dead are mourned.

"Mourner's Bench" was a particularly moving solo danced by Talley Beatty, which he finally revived for the Nanette Bearden Contemporary Dance Theater in the 1980s. Dancers who appeared in the Beatty company during these years included Ann Moon, Pat Connor, Jacqueline Freeman, Lew Smith and Arthur Wright.

A very important aspect of Talley Beatty's development as a choreographer whose sensitivity to music is extraordinary, was his association with Duke Ellington. They collaborated on several productions, including settings of the Ellington compositions *Black, Brown and Beige* and *A Drum is a Woman*, both for television, as well as other settings for the stage.

In 1959 Talley Beatty choreographed a work which excited both admiration and controversy, the *Road of the Phoebe Snow*. As to the meaning of the piece, Talley Beatty had this to say in his Hatch-Billups interview:

I think that the real problem – it never had program notes at first. And we did with that what all of my work deals with when I'm really down to something I want to really devote my time to, and that's alienation. If you have some kind of dramatic action for people to be

133

free – not to have to read program notes and say, now this is what they're doing here – but to get to respond to what's happening without having them programmed.

Explaining that he had acceded to program notes upon the insistence of Alvin Ailey, Beatty went on to explain:

> But those program notes had been, you know, the worst thing that could have happened as far as I'm concerned, because people tried to get to . . . you know, you go through an abstraction, the first thing is kind of literal and you can see the theme as anger or fighting against, you know, whatever this is that caused this kind of condition. So you see this always thrusting out and trying to break out of this situation.
>
> But the second one is just a poetic expression. It meant to me that, you know, no matter what you do to me here, this is what I really am. And each, all those little variations were people dancing.

None of Beatty's works can be reduced to literal meaning, in spite of the strong impress of contemporary life that each bears. Beatty himself, earlier in the Hatch-Billup interview, in response to a question about gesture, said,

> I am a little embarrassed by gesture. And I do have some gesture in "Phoebe," I guess. My wish is to be able to make the statement in terms of design and to extend the idea past a natural gesture. But, it has to come out of that. But that's my problem now. I just walked out of my rehearsal this afternoon because it's difficult. I prefer no gesture. But, it has to be an extension of that. How can you get it in design? But they do get it in design. You can get it in design. I know Alvin Nikolais. Now they say that he's dehumanizing, but I feel very strong emotional responses from some of that stuff he does, some of those theatrical things . . .
>
> And it makes dancers rather uncomfortable.

Major ballets by Talley Beatty include the following: *Road of the Phoebe Snow* (also known as *Route of the Phoebe Snow*) (1959), *Congo Tango Palace* (1960), *Montgomery Variations* (1967), *Toccata* (1969), *Caravanserai* (1971), *The Stack Up* (1983), and *Blues Shift* (1984).

Beatty has choreographed a considerable number of dramatic and musical works for Broadway and off-Broadway. These shows include: *The Blacks* (1961), *Fly, Blackbird* (1962), *Ballad for Bimshire* (1963), *House of Flowers* (revival, 1968), and *Don't Bother Me, I Can't Cope* (1970).

Donald McKayle

Donald McKayle is a classic product of the American modern dance. He studied at the New Dance Group and then with Martha Graham and Merce Cunningham, fixing him firmly in the tradition of modern dance. As a dancer he performed with Anna Sokolow, Graham, and Cunningham. He was following a "classic" modern dance pattern in making a Broadway appearance in *Bless You All* (1950), choreographed by Helen Tamiris. Subsequently his career has embraced fully both the concert and the theatrical worlds.

Organizing his own company in 1951, McKayle choreographed *Games*,

The Stack Up *performed by the Alvin Ailey American Dance Theater, 1986.*

an enduring staple of the concert world, since staged by many companies. An evocation of the lives of children in the impersonal city, *Games* is performed to songs and chants McKayle himself recalled from New York's streets. He turned to the story of the Underground Railroad's Harriet Tubman for the subject of *Her Name Was Harriet* (1952) and in 1959 produced from the lore of the chain gang another frequently performed work, *Rainbow 'Round My Shoulder*. The interaction of low life and the growth of jazz provided the subject of *District Storyville* (1962), a work later revived for the Alvin Ailey American Dance Theater. The Ailey company also premiered McKayle's ambitious *Blood Memories* (1976), an evocation of three rivers significant in the Black experience.

A major portion of McKayle's time and creative energy has gone into choreographing theatrical works. He worked as an assistant choreographer on *Redhead* (1959), whose dances were designed by Bob Fosse. In the theater McKayle is well remembered as the director and choreographer of the musical *Raisin* (1974), based on Lorraine Hansberry's *Raisin in the Sun*. His achievement with this musical received nearly unanimous applause. In 1964 he had been responsible for the choreography of *Golden Boy*, a musical starring Sammy Davis, Jr. An incomplete listing of other plays and musicals with which McKayle has been associated would show the following; *The Tempest* (1962), *As You Like It* (1963), *Trumpets of the Lord* (1963), *Time for Singing* (1964), *Black New World* (1967), *Doctor Jazz* (1975), *The Last Minstrel Show* (1978), and *Sophisticated Ladies* (1981).

McKayle was also the choreographer for the Disney film, *Bedknobs and Broomsticks* (1970), starring Angela Lansbury.

Carmen de Lavallade and Donald McKayle in Rainbow 'Round My Shoulder, *1963.*

A statement made by Donald McKayle to the inveterate dance interviewer John Gruen in the course of an interview published in *The New York Times* (November 4, 1973) effectively summarizes his own philosophy and the way he is perceived by colleagues and the public:

> I always begin a project with the knowledge that I am dealing with people – with individuals, with human beings. And my approach is always visceral. I give movements that are visceral. Everything must come from within. And everything must have meaning. When I choreograph, I never use people merely to create a design. I mean, abstraction is always present in an art form, and I use it, but I have never used human beings simply as a design element. My work has always been concerned with humanity, in one way or another. Basically, I feel the beauty in man is in his diversity, and in his deep inner feelings.

Donald McKayle's District Storyville, *AAADT, 1979.*

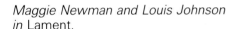
Maggie Newman and Louis Johnson in Lament.

Louis Johnson

Beginning dance studies in Washington, D.C., in the studios of the Jones-Haywood School, after already demonstrating considerable skill in acrobatics, Louis Johnson advanced so rapidly that after only one year his mentors brought him to New York, along with fellow student Chita Rivera, to audition for the School of American Ballet. He was accepted and, after finishing high school in Washington, returned to New York where he took classes at SAB as well as at the Katherine Dunham School. He was recruited as a guest artist for the New York City Ballet premiere of Robbins's *Ballade* (1952), but this did not lead to further work with the company.

Johnson choreographed his first ballet, *Lament*, in 1953 and immediately attained widespread recognition for his precocious talent. Shortly thereafter Johnson organized the first of the succession of companies with which he has been associated, largely for the presentation of his works. In 1960, on tour, the Louis Johnson Dance Company featured five pieces by Johnson: *Folk Impression*, *Olé* (solo), *Harlequin* (solo), *First Sin*, and *Trio*. Dancers on this tour were Thelma Hill, Delores Brown, Gene Sagan, Ronald Platts, and James Fairfax. Other dancers who appeared with Johnson during this period were Georgia Collins, Barbara Wright and Harold Pierson.

Intermittently Johnson appeared in Broadway shows, making a spectacular impact in the stage musical *Damn Yankees* (1955) and later in the film. He had previously appeared in Broadway in *My Darlin' Aida* (1952) and in *House of Flowers* (1954). In 1960 he was assistant choreographer for the musical, *Jamaica*, which starred Lena Horne. Subsequently Johnson has choreographed many shows for summer stock and regional theaters, as well as several Broadway musicals, including *Purlie* (1970), and the films *Cotton Comes to Harlem* (1970), and *The Wiz* (1978).

Johnson's work has been represented in the repertory of the Dance Theatre of Harlem by *Forces of Rhythm*, and in that of the Alvin Ailey company, by the immensely popular *Fontessa and Friends*.

Louis Johnson in Harlequin, *1960.*

Like many choreographers of his generation, Johnson has also choreographed for the stage acts of pop stars, including the Temptations and Aretha Franklin.

Louis Johnson's work draws on his ballet background as well as on more contemporary techniques from the modern and jazz vocabularies. The mix has not always been to the taste of critics. In mood, Johnson's ballets have run the gamut from the social protest, yet romantic, character of *No Way Out* (1968) to the humor of *When Malindy Sings* in which verses of Paul Laurence Dunbar alternate with danced incarnations of Lena Horne, Leontyne Price, Nina Simone, and Roberta Flack.

A wide-ranging figure in the world of dance, Louis Johnson has choreographed operas such as *Aida* for the Metropolitan Opera and *Treemonisha* for the Houston Opera and Broadway. He has been associated as an artistic director with the D. C. Black Repertory Company, along with Mike Malone; with the Negro Ensemble Company; and in the mid-1980s, as resident choreographer, he organized a dance company at the Henry Street settlement in New York City.

Louis Johnson's Forces of Rhythm, *Dance Theatre of Harlem, 1972.*

The Ailey Company: April Berry and Keith McDaniel in Fontessa and Friends.

Eleo Pomare

In 1988 Eleo Pomare commemorated thirty years of a confrontational career in dance. Though he was born in the Colombian port city of Cartagena, and as a child lived in the Caribbean island of San Andres and in Panama, he had reached Manhattan by age 10, and his absorption of Black life in that milieu has strongly marked his work, though elements of his Hispanic heritage often surface in his work as well. After graduating from the High School of the Performing Arts in New York, he began his commitment to working with other dancers by forming a company in 1958. He went to Europe on a fellowship in 1962, and had a brief turbulent period of study with the dance pioneer, Kurt Jooss, and then with other "expressionist" teachers in Holland. He organized a performing group in Amsterdam in 1964 to express his own burgeoning ideas, and in 1965 returned to New York where he began phase three of his career as choreographer and company director.

His earliest continuously performed piece is the somewhat austere *Cantos From a Monastery* (1958), a solo to the music of Alan Hovhaness. In 1965 he choreographed both the liturgical *Missa Luba* and the disturbing *Blues for the Jungle*. At the time of a 1984 performance of this work the critic Zita Allen wrote, in the *Amsterdam News* of November 24:

> While Eleo Pomare's choreography ranges from lush, lyrical abstractions with an exquisite sense of structure and musicality to potent dance-dramas about socio-political issues, his reputation has most often been associated with the latter. And with good reason.

Eleo Pomare in Blues for the Jungle, *1972.*

After recalling the period in which the piece was choreographed and the tensions which ensued from the creation of such "raw" works, Allen continued:

> Pomare's piece, "Blues for the Jungle," is one of the American dance masterpieces born of this era. From the opening scene of a shackled figure writhing on an auction block to its depiction of contemporary street scenes peopled with bitter, bewigged whores, pimps, bagmen, ladies, "Blues" is a montage of man's inhumanity to man.

She then went on to note the difficulties experienced by dancers half a generation later in capturing the spirit of such a piece.

Two psychologically thrilling works emerged in the late 1960s. These were the solo *Narcissus Rising* (1968), with its evocation of the bike culture and overtones of sado-masochism, and the insistent *Las Desenamoradas* (1967) (based on Garcia Lorca's *The House of Bernarda Alba*).

During his much-praised twenty-fifth anniversary season at the Joyce Theater in 1983, Pomare presented eleven works of his own creation, as well as guest works by Anna Sokolow, Thomas Pinnock, and George Faison. Pomare premieres included *Back to Bach*, in the "musicalized" tradition, and *Local Stops on a Full Moon*, a mellowed work of his realistic tradition. The performers included dancers long associated with Pomare, such as Charles Grant, Robin Becker, Andrea Borak, Quentin Clark, and Craig Moore. Well-known dancers new to the company for this season were Gina Ellis, Deborah Redd, and Thomas Reid. The immensely

Eleo Pomare's Las Desenamoradas *with (left to right) Jeanette Rollins, Judy Dearing, Delores Vanison, Shawneeque Baker-Scott, 1962.*

talented Dyane Harvey also participated in the season, dancing in several of Pomare's works as well as in those by Sokolow, Pinnock and Faison.

Gus Solomons, Jr.

Gus Solomons, Jr. must be numbered among the most analytical and cerebral personalities who appeared on the American dance scene in the 1960s. While his work fits comfortably within the climate of experimentation which characterized the ''post-modern'' dance scene, it is quite distinct from the direction favored by most Black choreographers and dancers during that decade and later.

Solomons studied architecture at the Massachusetts Institute of Technology; concurrently with his degree studies in architecture, he pursued studies in dance, both modern and ballet. He became a member of Dance Makers, a company in his native Boston, and there began his experiments in solo choreography.

After coming to New York in 1962, he shared a studio with a number of other dance innovators, whose collective and individual efforts came to be known as Studio 9. His highly esteemed skills as a dancer led him to work with a number of outstanding groups including the companies of Martha Graham, Joyce Trisler, Pearl Lang, and Donald McKayle. His longest and most significant involvement was with the Merce Cunningham Company, in which he danced from 1965 to 1968, leaving after an injury. In 1971, he founded his own company and has carved out a distinct niche in the world of dance.

Solomon's choreography has moved through explorations of

Gus Solomons, Jr.

geometry to the role of chance in movement to game forms. Speech and synthesized music have been essential ingredients of some of his compositions and his recital programs have proposed what he has referred to as "kinetic autobiography." He has avoided content and message and the creation of set repertory works intended to "endure." In an interview, he has stated:

> What I am trying to do – why I choreograph – is to find the most appropriate structure in which to display the dancing and dancers I have selected. The choreography is the frame rather than the source. I enjoy all the subtleties, the rough edges, the awkwardness that make the movement fresh. So that's my material. Then I have to find a way to put that out there for the audience to appreciate. That's why I make structures, and that's why I think that the structure and the content can be partially independent of each other.

Enlarging on this, in the same interview, he added:

> My concern is with the movement: its relation to itself and what the dancers feel as they do it. It will project something to the audience. Let the audience bring their own experiences and needs to it and it will satisfy them in their own way: It's like a buffet. I want them to fantasize for themselves.
>
> That may be where I'm on shaky ground: I do recognize that all movement has implication, but I don't feel the need to define those implications or explore them.

Solomons has maintained his experimental and pure aesthetic with far more persistence than other dancers of his talents and gifts. However, he was pained not to have been asked to participate in the "comprehensive" Dance Black America program at the Brooklyn Academy of Music in 1983, and wrote an open letter to the directors of that event in which he stated:

> I have spent twenty years making dances that stem from my honest experience and my perception of dance as an expression of energy-as-motion, not as a vehicle for the expression of racial anger or social oppression, which, fortunately, do not happen to be part of my personal background. It saddens me to realize, if indeed it is the case, that my work is apparently being ignored by my Black colleagues because it refuses ethno-cultural categorizing.

Gus Solomons, Jr. served as Dean of the Dance School at the California Institute of the Arts, but found that this distracted him from his central concern with choreography and performance. Since 1980, he has devoted some of his time to dance criticism, his reviews having appeared in *The Village Voice*, *Ballet News*, and *Attitude*, among other publications.

The experimental and often fugitive nature of the works created by Solomons makes it difficult to single out specific pieces. However, some of his works have been choreographed specifically for television and it is likely that audio-visual recording will be the medium of choice as the record of his works rather than their maintenance in repertory in a company of constantly changing interpreters.

Charles Grant in Pomare's Morning Without Sunrise, *1986.*

(Opposite above) Alvin Ailey flyer.

(Opposite) Alvin Ailey.

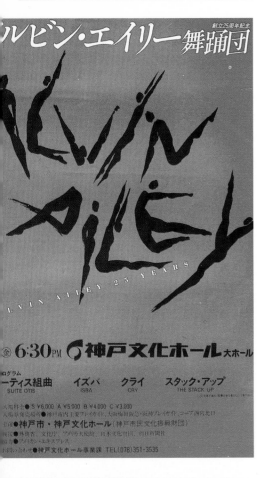

Alvin Ailey

The name which has come both to symbolize and encapsulate the Black presence in contemporary dance is that of Alvin Ailey. Sometimes rebuked by critics for slickness and show-business propensities, a charge often made in rancor and resentment, the artistic enterprise of Alvin Ailey has become the best-known expression of American dance in the world.

Dancer and Choreographer

Alvin Ailey, born in Texas, came to California at an early age but he has employed his "Southern" background in his most famed works. Athletic in person and in interests, he describes his predilection for dance as being awakened by a high-school performance by the young Carmen de Lavallade, a dancer with whom he was to enjoy a long and fruitful collaboration. His dance interests were reinforced by seeing a performance of the Katherine Dunham Company. As a company and school director Ailey was to contribute directly and decisively to the continuing of the Dunham heritage. Ailey's own development as a dancer is due chiefly to the tutelage and example of Lester Horton, the best known of the West Coast pioneers of American modern dance.

Among dancers and teachers associated with Horton were Maudelle, Bella Lewitsky, James Truitte, Joyce Trisler, and of course Ailey and de Lavallade. Due chiefly to Ailey's influence, the Horton technique is taught at many dance schools in New York and elsewhere. After Horton's death in late 1953 Ailey and other dancers in the Horton school and company sought to keep the enterprise going, but without success; it was during this period that Ailey choreographed two pieces which set him on his road as a choreographer, *Creation of the World* (Milhaud) and *Work Songs*. In the summer of 1954, Ailey led the Horton company in a Jacob's Pillow appearance which met with a less than enthusiastic reception.

In 1954 Ailey and de Lavallade both appeared as dancers in the film version of *Carmen Jones*. Later that year when Herbert Ross, one of the dance directors of the film, inherited the responsibility of preparing *House of Flowers* for Broadway he invited the California dancers to New York. Ailey took advantage of his presence in New York to sample the teaching of as many outstanding figures as possible, including the eminent moderns, Graham, Humphrey, Weidman and Holm, as well as Karel Shook for ballet.

In John Gruen's *The Private World of Ballet*, Ailey describes the period following the close of *House of Flowers* and the founding of his company:

Even though I starved a lot, I became immersed in the dance world. Then, in 1957, I landed a job in the Lena Horne musical *Jamaica*, and Jack Cole, who choreographed it, became an idol. He blew my mind completely. He was the first man since Lester Horton that completely knocked me over. Anyway, after a while, I decided to give a joint concert at the YMHA — on Ninety-second Street. A friend of mine, Ernest Parham, and I gathered together thirty-five of the most incredible dancers in New York, and we gave eight concerts in March 1958. I did *Blues Suite* and some Latin dances, and a solo dedicated to Lester Horton that I danced myself. So those were our first concerts in New York, and they were very successful. We received very good notices from John Martin of *The New York Times*. Then, I decided the next time I would give a concert on my own – which I did, in 1959, again at the "Y." Then I gave two more concerts, and by 1960, I was ready to form my own company.

Among the dancers who collaborated with Ailey in these early years were Minnie Marshall, James Truitte, Thelma Hill, Loretta Abbott, Ella Thompson, Charles Moore, Liz Williamson, Nat Horne, Lucinda Ransome, Audrey Mason, Georgia Collins, Myrna White, Joan Derby, and Merle Derby.

It was in 1960 that Ailey presented the first versions of *Revelations*, which became the signature piece of the company and one of the most renowned dance compositions of the century. *Revelations* was the second in a series of works devoted to elements of the Black heritage. The first, *Blues Suite*, had been the hit of the YMHA concerts in 1958. *Revelations*, based on the Black religious heritage, was presented to choral interpretations of spirituals. The third work was never brought to completion.

Revelations has evolved over the years, with various dancers putting a distinct mark on various sections. As presented by the Ailey company for many years, the composition has the following program:

PILGRIM OF SORROW
I Been Buked
Didn't My Lord Deliver Daniel
Fix Me Jesus

TAKE ME TO THE WATER
Processional
Wading in the Water
I Want To Be Ready

MOVE, MEMBERS, MOVE
Sinner Man
The Day is Past and Gone
You May Run On
Rocka My Soul in the Bosom of Abraham

The tripartite movement of the ballet is from dejection to regeneration to jubilation. The intense interplay of music and movement, which at some points touches upon literalism, is ultimately the greatest source of strength for this virtually indestructible monument of dance. Ailey has, understandably, from time to time expressed frustration with the public's unending demand for *Revelations*, but it has never been retired from the repertory and is now danced by the second Ailey company which, founded in 1974, has become an important touring organization. The influence of *Revelations* has been wide reaching (and uninspired imitations have been seen in the repertories of provincial companies).

During the first decade of the company's existence Ailey created over twenty ballets for company performance. Conspicuous among those in addition to *Blues Suite* and *Revelations* were: *Hermit Songs* (Barber; 1961), *Reflections in D* (Ellington; 1962), *Labyrinth* (Rosenthal; 1963), *The Twelve Gates* (folk; 1964), and *Quintet* (various composers; 1968).

In 1962 Ailey choreographed a ballet, *Feast of Ashes*, based on Lorca's *The House of Bernarda Alba*, for the Joffrey Ballet Company. In 1965 he choreographed *Ariadne* (Jolivet) for the Harkness ballet, following this up

Carmen de Lavallade in Letter to a Lady, *John Butler, 1960.*

Loretta Abbott in Blues Suite, *1964.*

James Truitte and Minnie Marshall in Revelations, *1963*.

the next year with two other ballets for the same company: *Macumba* (Harkness) and *El Amor Brujo* (de Falla). Subsequent major ballets by Alvin Ailey for his own company have been *Masakela Langage* (1969), *Streams* (1970), *Cry* (1971), *The Lark Ascending* (1972), *Love Songs* (1972), and *Memoria* (1974).

Ailey has also done the choreography for major opera productions; in 1966 he received the distinction of being asked to choreograph the opening production of the new Lincoln Center home of the Metropolitan Opera, Samuel Barber's *Antony and Cleopatra*, and in 1973 he choreographed a new production of *Carmen* for the Metropolitan.

Fairly early in his career Ailey turned, as had Talley Beatty, to the music of Duke Ellington as a source for choreographic work. In 1962 he created a piece, *Reflections in D*, to an Ellington piece and the next year he choreographed *First Negro Centennial* to an Ellington composition. In 1964 two works of Talley Beatty's, *Congo Tango Palace* (1969) and *The Road of the Phoebe Snow* (1959), both to Ellington-Strayhorn scores, entered the repertory of the Ailey company and a third Beatty/Ellington piece, *The Black Belt*, was added in 1967.

Ailey's ambitious project, "Ailey Celebrates Ellington," was to become a series of nine works based on Ellington scores, six entering the repertory in 1974 and three in 1976, these pieces by Ailey being supplemented by the works of other choreographers to Ellington's music. The most popular of these Ailey/Ellington works were two from 1974, *Night Creatures* and *The Mooche*, and two from 1976, *Black, Brown and Beige* and *Three Black Kings*.

The third work composed in 1976 was *Pas de Duke*, a special gala piece

145

The Ailey Company (above)
Revelations; *(below) Sara Yarborough
and Clive Thompson in* The Lark
Ascending, *1972;*

(opposite above)
Night Creatures, *1977; and (opposite
below) Donna Wood and Sarita Allen
in* Memoria.

The Ailey Company: (opposite)
Judith Jamison in The Mooche,
1975; (above) Suite Otis, 1977; (right)
Gary DeLoatch, April Berry, Rodney
Nugent in Katherine Dunham's
L'Ag'Ya.

designed to be danced by Judith Jamison and Mikhail Baryshnikov. It had a subsequent performance with Jamison and Mel Tomlinson, who was at that time a member of the company.

The Alvin Ailey Enterprise

By the mid-1970s Alvin Ailey's activities as a choreographer began, somewhat to his discomfort, to be engulfed both by his increasing stature as an artistic director, and by the demands upon him as the creative center of what can best be called the Ailey Enterprise.

There are three principal components which dominate the Alvin Ailey Enterprise. First and most visible is the Alvin Ailey American Dance Theater (AAADT); second, there is another company, the Alvin Ailey Repertory Ensemble; and third, there is the Alvin Ailey American Dance Center.

As a result of Ailey's basic generosity and openness of spirit, AAADT was very early developed into a repertory performing group. In all, more than 150 works by 45 choreographers have been performed by the company in three decades of existence.

Among the outstanding Black choreographers whose works have been figured in the repertory are Beatty, McKayle, Pomare, Louis Johnson, Billy Wilson, George Faison, Ulysses Dove, and Bill T. Jones, as well as Katherine Dunham and Pearl Primus. Company members whose choreography has been presented include John Parks, Kelvin Rotardier, Milton Myers, Gary DeLoatch, and Judith Jamison.

The Ailey Company in Choral Dances, *1971.*

The Ailey Company: Judith Jamison in Cry, *1976.*

The Ailey company has been presented in 48 states and in 45 countries, having visited all continents. This is a record unparalleled by any other performing arts institution.

The number of dancers who have appeared with AAADT in three decades approaches 250 and, though primarily Black American, the roster includes dancers of many different ethnic groups. Among "star" dancers with greater or lesser periods of prominence in the company may be numbered Judith Jamison, Dudley Williams, Clive Thompson, Donna Wood and Gary DeLoatch, as well as Marilyn Banks, Mary Barnett (later associate artistic director), George Faison, Miguel Godreau, Keith Lee, Keith McDaniel, Michelle Murray, Mel Tomlinson, Sylvia Waters, and Sara Yarborough.

The Alvin Ailey Repertory Ensemble was established in 1974. Both a training and performing company, it has supplied many of the dancers for AAADT as well as for other dance organizations. From its origins, under the direction of Sylvia Waters, the company has built up an independent repertory, some of it consisting of especially commissioned works, and a wide touring schedule. By December 1988 the company had had more than one hundred members, some thirty of whom went on to AAADT. Other "graduates" are to be found in theater and film, as well as in such companies as that of Martha Graham, Dance Theatre of Harlem, and the Hamburg ballet.

In addition to works of Alvin Ailey, both well-known and lesser-known ones, the company has performed choreography by Beatty, Rotardier, Dianne McIntyre, Myers, Solomons, Fred Benjamin, Mary Barnett, McKayle, Keith Lee, and George Faison.

The Alvin Ailey American Dance Center (AAADC), the official school of the Ailey organization, grew out of classes conducted in 1969 in Brooklyn; the next year the growing operation was moved to Manhattan, where it shared quarters with the classes conducted by the distinguished modern dance choreographer, Pearl Lang, in connection with her company. Within a year the two choreographers had begun to coordinate their efforts, and a full range of dance offerings was made available to a growing student body.

With Alvin Ailey and Pearl Lang as artistic directors, the AAADC has been under the active direction of Denise Jefferson, a dancer with broad educational experience in the dance, for several years. The faculty has included, at various times, Delores Brown, Walter Raines, Lavinia Williams, Pearl Reynolds, Kelvin Rotardier, Sylvia Waters, Miguel Godreau, and Joe Nash, as well as active members of the Alvin Ailey American Dance Theater.

The Alvin Ailey American Dance Center attracts students from all over the United States and from abroad, and offers an accredited certificate program in dance. The curriculum includes ballet, Dunham technique,

Kelvin Rotardier.

The Ailey Company in Pigs and Fishes, *1982.*

Sylvia Waters.

(Above right) The Ailey Company: Dudley Williams in Caravan, *1976.*

The Ailey Company: Sarita Allen in Treading.

Horton technique, jazz and modern, as well as courses in dance history and dance competition.

The Dance Theatre of Harlem

Nurtured by the optimism and idealism of the Civil Rights Era, the rapid emergence and early success of the Dance Theatre of Harlem (DTH) is attributable almost totally to the remarkable skills and personality of Arthur Mitchell who, together with the dedicated white ballet teacher Karel Shook, founded the company in 1969. A year earlier Mitchell had begun teaching ballet classes at the Harlem School of the Arts. The success of this enterprise, and an inevitable conflict with the music-oriented program of the school's founder-director Dorothy Maynor, led to an independent school and company. In the establishment of this new enterprise, Mitchell's determination and charm were aided by the social and political climate, and a certain sense of relief of finding himself in a dance establishment which could now contribute talent and material support to Black ballet in the form of a distinct and separate company.

Dancers for the initial seasons of the company were recruited widely, and the early roster included such established performers as John Jones, James Thurston, Sheila Rohan, and Walter Raines, as well as the prodigious Sara Yarborough. DTH made its first appearance at the Jacob's Pillow Dance Festival in the summer of 1969. In the seasons that followed, the company developed a diverse repertory which it presented in a heavy and increasingly international touring schedule.

In a retrospective critique in the mid-1980s Anna Kisselgoff, chief dance critic of *The New York Times*, spoke of the repertory of the company, distinguishing seven categories:

1) The Balanchine tradition. This includes such works of Balanchine as *Serenade, Agon*, and *Bukagu*, as well as works by such Balanchine associates as John Taras and Arthur Mitchell himself (*Holberg Suite*).

2) The Ballet Russe tradition. Ballets such as *Schéhérazade*, and Act II of *Swan Lake*.

153

Arthur Mitchell.

Walter Raines and Llanchie Stevenson in Tones, *DTH, 1971.*

Karel Shook, cofounder of Dance Theatre of Harlem.

Eddie J. Shellman and Judy Tyrus in Le Corsaire, *DTH, 1989.*

Lowell Smith and Virginia Johnson in A Streetcar Named Desire, *DTH, 1983.*

3) The Black Heritage. A category which includes ballets of Geoffrey Holder such as *Dougla*.

4) Contemporary Fusion. Represented by choreographers such as Glen Tetley and Billy Wilson (*Concerto in F*).

5) Bravura pieces. The pas de deux from *Le Corsaire* illustrates this category.

6) Modernist revival pieces. Such as Bronislava Nijinka's *Les Biches*.

7) Dance drama. Agnes de Mille's *Fall River* and Valerie Bettis's *A Streetcar Named Desire* are in this category.

Two of the most spectacular productions of DTH have been its productions of *Firebird* and *Giselle*. Utilizing the 1945 version of the *Firebird* score by Stravinsky, John Taras fashioned a choreographic design which is in fact relatively simple, making strong technical demands only on the dancer doing the title role; the verve with which the company performs the work, abetted mightily by the brilliant costuming of Geoffrey Holder, has made the work a favorite with audiences. The two-act *Giselle* staged for DTH by Frederic Franklin moves the action of the ballet from a corner of the Rhine to a locale in antebellum Louisiana, where the class structure of a Black milieu provides a near-parallel to the setting of the original scenario.

Judy Tyrus, Karlya Shelton, Yvonne Hall, Terri Tompkins in Swan Lake, *DTH, 1980.*

Among dancers who have had long and distinguished careers with DTH are Sheila Rohan, Stephanie Dabney, Virginia Johnson, Lorraine Graves, Derek Williams, Walter Raines, Ronald Perry, Eddie J. Shellman, and Lowell Smith.

Lowell Smith, Mitchell McCarthy and company members in Troy Game, *DTH, 1989.*

Teachers

An impressive achievement in the teaching of dance has been recorded by a host of performers in the world of Black dance. The work of Katherine Dunham and Pearl Primus is canonical in this respect. Of dancers who were associated with Dunham at one time or another, a considerable number who have international reputations as teachers could be cited. These include:

Carmencita Romero, who has had schools or conducted classes in Cuba, Italy, Japan, Spain, and Germany.

Lavinia Williams, who, in addition to her work in Haiti, has taught in the Bahamas, Guyana, Jamaica, and Germany.

Vanoye Aikens, a faculty member of the Royal Swedish School of Dance for many years.

Walker Nicks, who taught in Scandinavia and in France.

Syvilla Fort, for many years one of the leading teachers in New York City.

The Dunham-related list can be expanded with the names of Wilbert Bradley, Claude Marchant, Tommy Gomez, Archie Savage, Ruth Beckford, Glory Van Scott, and Pearl Reynolds. Yet another Dunham dancer

Carmencita Romero, 1981, in Rome.

Glory Van Scott as Jezebel in Hughes' Prodigal Son, *Paris, 1965.*

Larry Phillips.

Marie Brooks Children's Dance Theater.

who has made a unique contribution to dance in New York, with a series of projects in children's dance theater, is Marie Brooks.

Clyde Morgan, a dancer trained with Daniel Nagrin, Olatunji, and others, and who became a soloist with the José Limón company, has had a considerable career in Brazil, teaching at the University of Bahia and organizing several performing groups.

One of the best-known dance teachers in New York was Thelma Hill, who performed with Ailey, Louis Johnson, and other major figures. Her death by accident in 1977 inspired the dancer Larry Phillips to create the Thelma Hill Performing Arts Center, and this has made significant contributions to Black dance history through a series of "celebratory" programs honoring the achievements of men and women. Phillips himself died in the late 1980s.

Repertory Companies

The example set by Alvin Ailey in including works by other choreographers in the repertory of his own company was an important one, and has been emulated in the setting-up of a number of companies on the repertory model. One of the most highly esteemed of these companies is the Dayton Contemporary Dance Company founded by Jeraldyne Blunden in 1968. Blunden, who had studied with Graham, Limón, and James Truitte, the eminent associate of Lester Horton and Alvin Ailey, had danced in Dayton's ballet company and had taught at several colleges. In 1988, its twentieth year, the Dayton Contemporary Dance

Company counted in its repertory over thirty works, including *The Road of the Phoebe Snow* (Talley Beatty), *Streams* (Alvin Ailey), *Liberian Suite* (James Truitte/Lester Horton), *Las Desenamoradas* (Eleo Pomare), and *Joplinesque* (Billy Wilson).

Billy Wilson.

In addition, the company presents works of its own choreographers including Kevin Ward, Debbie Blunden, and founder Jeraldyne Blunden.

The Philadelphia Dance Company, known as Phildanco, was founded by Joan Myers Brown in 1970. From its beginnings, Brown called upon outstanding figures in the Black dance world to assist in the development of the company and its associated school. Those who answered the call over the years include Walter Nicks, Talley Beatty, Louis Johnson, Gene Hill Sagan, and Harold Pierson. Pieces in the repertory include *Forces of Rhythm* and *Treemonisha* by Louis Johnson, and *Leilo* by Sagan.

The Cleo Parker Robinson Dance Ensemble was founded in Denver in 1971. Robinson, the founder, is a native of Denver and received most of her dance training in Colorado, some distance from role models in the Black dance world. She turned in building the repertory of the company, however, to a number of outstanding figures including Eleo Pomare, Rod

Dayton Contemporary Dance Company, Twentieth Anniversary Season, 1988–9.

Pomare's Las Desenamoradas *by the
Dayton Contemporary Dance
Company, American Dance Festival,
1988. Dancers: Debbie L. Blunden,
Dawn Wood, Sheri Williams, Shonna
Yvette Hickman, Karen Moon, Debra
Walton, Eric J. Miles, Blaine Evans,
Michael L. Groomes, Calvin Norris
Young.*

Fred Benjamin.

Phildanco: Evelyn Watkins.

Phildanco: Tom Myles, Deanna Murphy and Danielle Gee in Gene Hill Sagan's Ritornello.

Rodgers, Milton Myers, Donald McKayle, and Chuck Davis. *Raindance* by Myers has become a signature piece of the company.

Following her earlier initiatives in organizing dance events, in 1976 Nanette Rohan Bearden (actively encouraged by her husband, the artist Romare Bearden) created the Nanette Bearden Contemporary Dance Theater (NBCDT). The company was intended "to provide opportunity for young dancers and choreographers to work in comparative freedom — unfettered by commercial demands . . ."

Associated with Nanette Bearden over the years in the artistic direction of the company have been Gary DeLoatch, later a luminary of the Ailey company, Rick Odums, who subsequently continued his career in France, and Walter Rutledge. The company has presented choreography by Rutledge, DeLoatch, Odums, Otis Sallid, John Jones, and many others. A major project of the company was a series of works to the music of Mary Lou Williams, one of the most eminent figures of American jazz. The 1988 presentation, "Homage to Mary Lou," included new pieces by Talley Beatty, Fred Benjamin, Dianne McIntyre, and Walter Rutledge, and an excerpt from Ailey's *Mary Lou's Mass* (1971).

Sheila Rohan, well known as a dancer with the Dance Theatre of Harlem, was associated with NBCDT from its founding, as dancer and as ballet mistress. Among other dancers associated with the company have been Gina Ellis, Bruce Hawkins, and Roumel Reaux.

Cleo Parker Robinson Company in Milton Myers' Raindance, *1983.*

Cleo Parker Robinson.

164

Unitary Companies

Dance criticism has developed no satisfactory term to describe what is, in fact, the archetypal company model of the modern dance: the company organized by, directed by, and performing exclusively – or almost exclusively – the works of, a single choreographer or of two closely collaborating choreographers. The prototypes were the Martha Graham Company and the Humphrey-Weidman Company.

A number of Black-led one-choreographer or unitary companies flourished for longer or shorter periods well before the explosion of the late 1960s, including those of Beatty, McKayle, and Louis Johnson.

In 1967 the Rod Rodgers Dance Company made a decisive entrance on the dance scene and has maintained its position over a period of two decades. Particularly noted for his use of intricate rhythmic accompaniment, Rogers has built up a considerable repertoire which provides the performing agenda of his company. In addition, his works are included in the repertories of other companies. The Rodgers repertory "encompasses jazz ballets, sculptural movement landscapes, dance drama as probing social commentary and a unique series of contemporary Rhythmdances (where the performers contribute to the musical environment with hand-held instruments) . . ."

Rod Rodgers.

A 1988 program of the company presented the following pieces by Rodgers: *Rhythm Ritual* (1973), *Poets and Peacemakers* (Harriet Tubman), *Tangents* (1976), *El --- Encounter* (1988), and *In Hi-Rise Shadows* (1988).

Among dancers performing with the Rodgers company in 1988 was the veteran dancer, John Jones.

Two unitary companies, each of which has offered major innovations in content and movement in the 1970s and 1980s are Garth Fagan's Bucket Dance Company and the Bill T. Jones/Arnie Zane Company. The dance career of Garth Fagan began in Jamaica where he was a member of the Ivy Baxter Company. He was directly influenced in development by Pearl Primus and Lavinia Williams. Coming to New York, he studied with a number of modern dance giants such as Graham, Limón and Mary Hinkson. The Bucket Dance Company began as an inner-city dance project in Rochester, New York in 1970. The company that emerged under Fagan's direction provides an excellent medium for his abstract, intellectually potent, choreography. It has since performed on national tours. Fagan's increasingly complex choreography includes such pieces as *Prelude* (1983), *Oatka Tract* (1979), and a piece now consecrated as classic, *From Before* (1978).

Bill T. Jones, a virtuoso dancer, has choreographed solos for himself, and works for groups, both alone and in collaboration with Arnie Zane. Jones's choreography is basically abstract and episodic, but its inventiveness has invited popular esteem. *Fever Swamp* (1983), choreographed for

Rod Rodgers Company: Catherine Smith, Brendon Upson, and Kenneth Still in Against Great Odds, *1987.*

Garth Fagan.

Joel Hall Dancers: Angel Abcede, Elaine McLaurin, Duana Pendarvis, Vanessa Truvillion, Tracy Hodgkin-Valcy, Keith Perry in Nightwalker.

the Ailey company is also performed by the Jones/Zane company. A later work by Jones for the Ailey company was *How to Walk An Elephant* (1985).

The Joel Hall Dancers of Chicago is a company founded in Chicago in 1974 which, originally dancing almost exclusively works by the founder, has begun to develop in the direction of a repertory company. Hall's style has been described by Jennifer Dunning as "a fairly even mix of jazz dance, modern dance, and ballet." The company has found a genuinely enthusiastic audience in Britain, doing four tours there in three years beginning in 1985.

All of the unitary companies mentioned above have ethnically diverse rosters of dancers, as do the older companies of Eleo Pomare and Gus Solomons.

Smaller-scale companies on the model indicated above are those of Dianne McIntyre (Sounds in Motion), Bebe Miller, and Urban Bush Women, all of whom warrant more extended treatment. Of interest, too, are the often solo enterprises of experimentalists such as Blondell Cummings and Ishmael Houston-Jones.

Joel Hall Dancers: Elaine McLaurin and Vanessa Truvillion in Talley Beatty's Congo Tango Palace, *1988.*

Jazz, Tap, and Beyond

Writing in *Dance Magazine* (February 1978) in collaboration with Mike Moore, the distinguished dancer and teacher Liz Williamson noted:

> All over the world interest in jazz dance is burgeoning. More students than ever are studying jazz forms. Teachers are eager to find out more about this rich branch of the art. The audience for jazz dance increases each year. The questions about jazz are never-ending. And the misconceptions and preconceptions that people have about jazz dance seem numberless.

The article reveals in its episodic survey how broad and complicated the category of jazz dance is. Liz Williamson, a dancer of wide-ranging experience, is at once a historian and an exponent of the world of jazz dance. Another aspect of vernacular or jazz dance is represented by Pepsi Bethel, whose roots lie in the Savoy Ballroom traditions of virtuosic couple dancing. And yet another is reflected in the career of the tap maestro Henry Le Tang, who has choreographed many Broadway shows. Each of these personalities has had a great impact on the world of jazz dance.

The ongoing influence of tap has been reflected in Broadway shows such as the *Tap Dance Kid* (1983), which starred the dancer Hinton Battle, also an accomplished ballet dancer. In the late 1980s, older dancers such as Honi Coles and Sammy Davis, Jr., and younger dancers such as Maurice and Gregory Hines, have all been featured in a variety of settings which pay tribute to the vitality of the tap tradition.

A pop tradition in dance surfaced in 1960 with Chubby Checker (Ernest Evans) and the twist. Chubby Checker himself appeared in several "twist" films, before the craze subsided. It was followed by the break dance craze, which exploded in the early 1970s, spawning its own films somewhat later.

Tap Dance Kid.

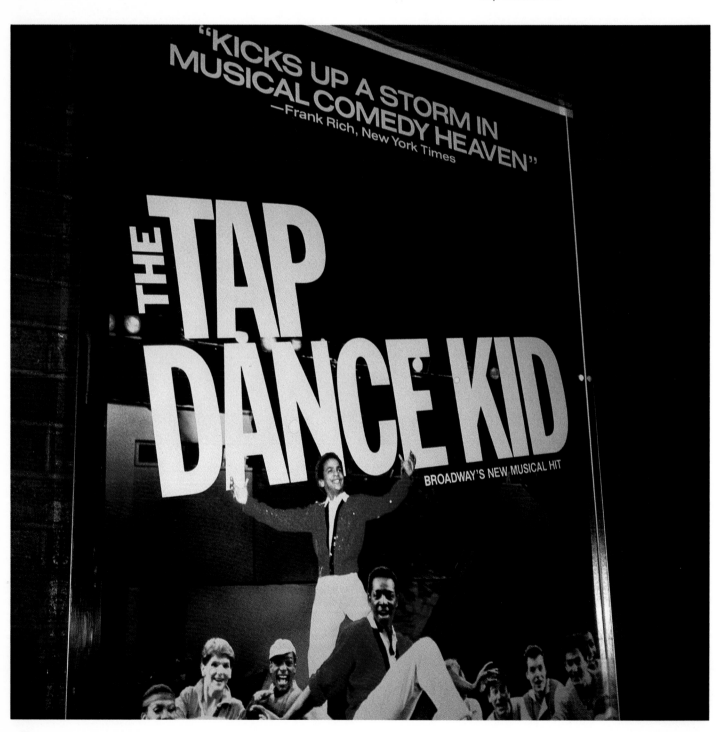

Liz Williamson.

In the world of pop dancing there has probably been no figure more applauded and emulated than Michael Jackson, whose "Moonwalk" and other dance exploits, in conjunction with his singing, have become a major cultural source. Pop dancing in the Jackson mode is indebted to serious choreographic invention from the Black tradition in modern dance, as are the choreographed routines of other pop singers.

Television and video have brought a number of Black dancers to the fore, particularly Debbie Allen and Gene Ray of the television series *Fame*. Among choreographers for this popular series was Mike Malone.

"A Gala Celebration of 50 Years of Men in Dance," April 14, 1980. Top, left to right: Ward Flemyng, Lenwood Morris, Randolph Sawyer, Honi Coles, Al Bledger. Center, left to right: John Hines, Joe Nash, Dinizulu. Bottom, left to right: Tommy Gomez, Fayard Nicholas, Harold Nicholas.

The Jamaica Connection

Like Haiti and Trinidad, Jamaica has contributed to and interacted with the Black dance scene in the United States, though entering the picture at a later point. Among important dancers born and partly trained in Jamaica who have become actively identified with dance in the United States, the most notable are Clive Thompson and Garth Fagan, both of whom have developed performing companies. Other dancers include Derek Williams of the Dance Theatre of Harlem and Thomas Pinnock, who was a member of the Rod Rodgers Company.

In her book *The Arts of an Island*, devoted to "the folk and creative arts in Jamaica 1494–1962," the dancer-choreographer Ivy Baxter pays ample tribute to Hazel Johnston, who had studied dance in England and returned to teach and choreograph dances in Jamaica. Johnston's brief career (1937–44) resembled that of many Black dance teachers in the United States, such as Essie Marie Dorsey of Philadelphia. Ivy Baxter herself, however, was inspired by the example of Beryl McBurnie of Trinidad (as well as by her own visits to the Jamaican countryside to observe dances such as the Kumina dance of St. Thomas Parish) and organized the first "modern" dance troupe in Jamaica. The Ivy Baxter Dance Group thrived for ten years between 1950 and 1960, and included among its members Eddy Thomas, Eyrick Darby, Roman Critchlow, Clive Thompson, Garth Fagan, and Rex Nettleford. (Baxter subsequently studied dance in London with Sigurd Leeder of the Kurt Jooss Ballet, and taught at the University of Toronto for two years.)

In 1961, under the direction of Rex Nettleford and Noel Vaz (staff tutor in drama at the University of the West Indies) and utilizing dancers from several companies, the "Dance Theatre Group" performed at Howard University in Washington and at Morgan State College in Baltimore; the collaboration of the folklorist-poet-actress Louise Bennett was important in this venture. This enthusiastically received production, *Sun Over the West Indies*, included as dancers Ivy Baxter, Eddy Thomas, Rex Nettleford, Sheila Barnett, Joyce Campbell, Audley Butler, Yvonne Da Costa, Clive Thompson and Bert Rose. Choreography was notably by Ivy Baxter and Eyrick Darby. Musicians were the Frats Quartet and an orchestra led by Mapletoft Poulle. Following the galvanizing influence of this overseas "tour," dance activity in Jamaica increased in anticipation of the coming independence celebrations, for which a production *Roots and Rhythms* was mounted by Rex Nettleford and Eddy Thomas.

National Dance Theatre Company of Jamaica (NDTC)
NDTC was founded in 1962, in the wake of the Jamaican Independence celebrations, by Rex Nettleford and Eddy Thomas. Thomas, whose direct involvement with the company ceased in 1967 when he left to pursue other interests, was an acclaimed dancer and choreographer, who also possessed immense talent as a musician and designer. He contributed a number of works to the company's early repertory.

Nettleford has been associated with the company throughout its history; he has been artistic director, dancer, choreographer, theorist, spokesman, and historian. As well as giving numerous formal and informal talks and lectures, Nettleford has also written two books on the company and its relation to Jamaican culture and society. *Roots and*

Charles "Honi" Coles, winner of the Capezio Award "for utmost skill, irrepressible style and keeping the faith in the art of tap-dancing."

173

Abdel Salaam and Dyane Harvey in Coming Forth By Day, *1985.*

Rael Lamb in Mudbird, *1984.*

Rhythms (1969) and *Dance Jamaica* (1985), both with photographs by Maria LaYacona, form an extensive record of NDTC in all of its various activities in Jamaica, the Caribbean, and the larger world. Nettleford's reputation as a figure in the world of the dance is towering, but this is a single aspect of a truly remarkable career. After university studies in Jamaica he was a Rhodes Scholar at Oxford in politics, where he was active as a choreographer with the Oxford University Dramatic Society and other groups. Returning to Jamaica, he assumed a post at the University in Extramural Studies while also lecturing in politics. He has maintained an unbroken connection with the University of the West Indies, heading its Trade Union Institute, the Extramural Department, and participating in many University initiatives. He has also been a television commentator, Jamaican representative to many regional and international bodies, and Chairman of the Institute of Jamaica. In the realm of the dance, his choreographic activities have extended to the staging of many musical dramas, as well as to the construction of the greater part of the repertory of NDTC.

Dis Poem, *choreographed to the dub poetry of Mutabaruka by Rex Nettleford for principal dancers of the NDTC.*

Other company choreographers, in addition to cofounder Eddy Thomas, have included Sheila Barnett, Neville Block and Bert Rose. Guest choreographers have included John Jones, Clive Thompson and Edwardo Rivero of Cuba.

Following an outline proposed by Nettleford, the repertory of NDTC, which had included by 1988 approximately 120 works, has embodied the following categories:

    1) Social commentary
    2) The matriarchal presence
    3) The African presence
    4) Religion and ritual
    5) Ritual and legend
    6) Plantation America
    7) Explorations in dance movement

In Jamaica NDTC presents annual seasons in Kingston which have ranged from nine performances in 1962 to as many as 40 in recent years; in addition, performances in smaller towns, company lectures, and demonstrations are included in the company schedule. The company has also traveled widely in and out of the Caribbean not only to the United States, but also to Canada, Mexico, Venezuela, Britain, Germany, Russia, and Australia. Notable United States appearances have been several each

Love duet from One Time, *a work by Sheila Barnett, founding member of the NTDC.*

Rex Nettleford as the King in Kumina, *which he choreographed in 1971 for the NTDC.*

in New York and Miami, as well as a residency at Spelman College of the Atlanta University Center. In the Caribbean, its 1972 appearance at Carifesta in Georgetown, Guyana, was electrifying and galvanized several other Caribbean states to explore the possibility of creating similar companies.

Fundamental to the existence of the NDTC has been the voluntary nature of the contribution to national artistry and national pride made by all members of the company. No performer or other artistic participant receives pay. This is the only formula which would permit an impoverished nation such as Jamaica to sustain such an enterprise.

No more striking testimony of the dedication of NDTC to the national interest can be given than the events surrounding its gala performance at Kennedy Center in Washington, D.C. on September 18, 1988. This was a long-scheduled gala event, and it was fully subscribed weeks in advance by friends of the company and of Jamaica. However, only a few days before the performance, Hurricane Gilbert – the worst storm in a century – swept through Jamaica, leaving incalculable havoc, and destroying the company's theater and practice rooms; company members also suffered personal damages. Rex Nettleford succeeded in leaving Jamaica on the first flight that left the island after the storm, and the entire company followed within a few hours, presenting to an astonished Washington audience a full program without a single change.

This extraordinary feat by NDTC may well be considered a metaphor for the determination to dance, which has led to the Black tradition in dance as we have traced it in this book.

Barry Moncrieffe, principal dancer with the NTDC, rehearsing at Brooklyn College, New York, in 1987.

Chronology

1920   *Emperor Jones*   play by Eugene O'Neill

1921   *Shuffle Along*   musical comedy
     Juba (Shawn/Dett)   danced by Martha Graham and others

1922   *Strut Miss Lizzie*   musical comedy
     Liza   (Charleston introduced)

1923   *Running Wild*   musical comedy (includes tune "Charleston")

1924   *Dixie to Broadway*   revue with Florence Mills
     Chocolate Dandies   revue with Josephine Baker

1925   *The New Negro*   anthology edited by Alain Locke
     Revue Nègre   revue in Paris with Josephine Baker
     Crapshooter (Shawn)   danced by Charles Weidman

1926   "The Negro Artist and the Racial Mountain" manifesto by Langston Hughes
     Bill Robinson in vaudeville at the Palace
     Blackbirds   revue with Florence Mills (travels to London and Paris after Harlem opening)

1927   John Martin appointed dance critic of *The New York Times*
     Africana   revue with Ethel Waters

1928   Helen Tamiris dances *Negro Spirituals* (Nobody Knows De Trouble I See; Joshua Fit de Battle of Jericho) in her first solo concert
     Blackbirds of 1928   revue featuring Bill Robinson and "Snake Hips" Tucker
     Buddy Bradley begins teaching at the Billy Pierce studio

1929   *The Little Show*   revue featuring "Moanin' Low" danced by Clifton Webb, choreographed by Buddy Bradley
     Salome   with Hemsley Winfield
     Wonder Bar   revue with Al Jolson featuring Chilton and Thomas, dance duo
     Hallelujah   film with Nina Mae McKinney

1930   *The Green Pastures*   musical play
     Blackbirds of 1930   revue with Ethel Waters and Buck and Bubbles

     Go Down Death   danced by Esther Jungen (to a poem by James Weldon Johnson)
     Brown Buddies   revue with Bill Robinson

1931   New Negro Art Theater Dance Company founded by Hemsley Winfield
     Randolph Sawyer joins Dance Center
     "First Negro Dance Recital in America" (Hemsley Winfield, Edna Guy)
     Katherine Dunham founds Negro Dance Group (Chicago)

1932   *Voodoo Ceremonial* (Horton)
     Harlem is Heaven   film with Bill Robinson
     Let Freedom Ring   revue at Roxy with Hall Johnson Choir and Hemsley Winfield Group
     Great Day   musical play by Zora Neale Hurston with Bahama Dancers

1933   Edna Guy and Group at Harlem YWCA
     The Modern Dance by John Martin published
     Forum: "What Shall the Negro Dance About?"
     Run Little Chillun by Hall Johnson, choreographed by Doris Humphrey, with Bahama Dancers
     Negro Spirituals (Shawn) danced by Shawn's Male Dancers
     Emperor Jones   film
     Emperor Jones   opera at Metropolitan with Winfield and group
     La Guiablesse (Ruth Page/William Grant Still), based on Martinican tale by Lafcadio Hearn, Ruth Page soloist, at Chicago Civic Opera

1934   *Four Saints in Three Acts*   opera by Virgil Thomson/ Gertrude Stein with all-Black cast, choreographed by Frederick Ashton
     Kykunkor   dance-drama by Asadata Dafora
     La Guiablesse (Page/Still)   with Katherine Dunham as soloist (Chicago)
     Kid Millions   film with Nicholas Brothers
     Edna Guy recital with Raymond Sawyer as guest artist

1935   Bill Robinson featured in five films
     Porgy and Bess   opera with John Bubbles
     Zouzou   film with Josephine Baker

1936 *Ziegfeld Follies of 1936* with Josephine Baker
The Jazz Decade (Shawn)
Macbeth all-Black Federal Theatre Production by Orson Welles, with African Dance Group directed by Asadata Dafora

1937 Negro Ballet directed by Eugene Von Grona at Lafayette Theatre
Negro Dance Evening at YMHA (Edna Guy, Allison Burroughs, Katherine Dunham, Asadata Dafora)
How Long, Brethren? (Tamiris/Negro Protest Songs), Federal Theatre Dance Unit Production
Candide (Weidman) Federal Theatre Dance Unit with Add Bates as General

1938 *Zuguru* dance-drama by Asadata Dafora
L'Ag'Ya (Dunham) first version (Chicago)
Bill Robinson in three films
Calabar Dancers at Brooklyn Museum
Wilson Williams recital at YMHA
Beryl McBurnie teaches at New Dance Group

1939 *Black Ritual* (also known as *Obeah*) choreographed by de Mille for Ballet Theatre with all-Black female cast
Pins and Needles Katherine Dunham choreographed 1939 version
The Swing Mikado musical play (originated in Chicago)
The Hot Mikado musical play featuring Bill Robinson
Swingin' the Dream musical play

1940 *Tropics* and *Le Jazz Hot* Katherine Dunham and troupe at Windsor Theatre
Cabin in the Sky musical comedy with Katherine Dunham and her dancers
A Trip Through the Tropics presented by Beryl McBurnie in Trinidad

1941 Jacob's Pillow Festival founded
Carnival of Rhythm film short featuring Dunham Company
Wilson Williams group appears at Humphrey-Weidman Studio Theater

1942 *Antilliana* presented by Beryl McBurnie (Belle Rosette)

1943 *Strange Fruit, Rock Daniel, Hard Times Blues* choreographed and danced by Pearl Primus
Pearl Primus at Café Society Downtown; Primus named Dance Debutante of the Year by John Martin
Carmen Jones opera (based on Bizet's *Carmen*) with all-Black cast
Tropical Revue concert-theatrical revue/recital by Katherine Dunham and troupe
African Dance Festival arranged by Asadata Dafora
Stormy Weather film with Bill Robinson, Dunham and troupe, Nicholas Brothers and Lester Horton Dancers

1945 *Memphis Bound* musical comedy with Bill Robinson and Avon Long
Carib Song dance-drama with Katherine Dunham and troupe and Avon Long
Katherine Dunham School opened
Study in Choreography film by Maya Deren with Talley Beatty

1946 *Show Boat* musical comedy revival with choreography by Tamiris. Dancers include Pearl Primus, Talley Beatty
St. Louis Woman musical comedy with Nicholas Brothers
Bal Negre concert-theatrical revue with Katherine Dunham and troupe
Journey to Accompong book by Katherine Dunham

1947 Hollywood Negro Ballet founded
Finian's Rainbow musical comedy with integrated dance company
The Medium opera by Menotti, featuring Leo Coleman in mime role
Caribbean Carnival revue choreographed by Pearl Primus

1948 American Dance Festival (ADF) founded at Connecticut College
Caribbean Rhapsody revue with Katherine Dunham and Company (London)
Little Carib Theatre founded by Beryl McBurnie (Trinidad)

1949 *Troubled Island* opera by William Grant Still at New York City Opera. Choreographed by Balanchine with company of Jean-Leon Destine

1950 *Out of This World* musical comedy choreographed by Hanya Holm, with Janet Collins as Night
Salome (Horton) with Carmen de Lavallade (Los Angeles)
Primus at ADF
Mambo film with Katherine Dunham Dancers

1951 *Games* (McKayle)
Primus on tour

1952 Mary Hinkson and Matt Turney join Martha Graham Company
Ronnie Aul at ADF

1953 Lavinia Williams goes to Haiti and opens school

1954 *Carmen Jones* film with dancers including Carmen de Lavallade and Alvin Ailey
House of Flowers musical comedy with distinguished group of dancers
Sheldon Hoskins and dance group at Carl Fischer Auditorium
Dunham School closed

1955   *Damn Yankees* musical comedy choreographed by Bob Fosse, featuring Louis Johnson in "Baseball Number"
Les Ballets Nègre directed by Ward Flemyng

1956   Arthur Mitchell at New York City Ballet
Negro Dance Theatre of Aubrey Hitchins at Jacob's Pillow
Mr Wonderful musical comedy with Sammy Davis, Jr.
Dunham Company tours to Pacific and East Asia

1957   New York Negro Ballet in Europe
Jamaica musical comedy choreographed by Jack Cole; Alvin Ailey lead dancer
Dunham company disbanded in Japan
Lament (Louis Johnson)

1958   Ballet Americana (formerly New York Negro Ballet) at YMHA
Pearl Primus guest artist with Percival Borde Company
Arthur Hill Afro-American Dance Ensemble founded (Philadelphia)
Ailey American Dance Theater founded
A Touch of Innocence book by Katherine Dunham published

1959   Primus and Borde go to Liberia
Road of the Phoebe Snow (Beatty)
Rainbow 'Round My Shoulder (McKayle)
Dunham company reformed (until 1962)

1960   Asadata Dafora goes to Sierra Leone
Revelations (Ailey)
Congo Tango Palace (Beatty)
The Figure in the Carpet (Balanchine) New York City Ballet (NYCB) with Mitchell and Mary Hinkson (guest artist)

1961   Capitol Ballet (directed by Doris Jones and Claire Haywood) founded (Washington, D.C.)
Sun Over the West Indies revue featuring Jamaican dancers in Washington and Baltimore
The Wedding (Primus)
Modern Jazz-Variants (Balanchine) NYCB with Mitchell and John Jones (guest artist)
Portrait of Billie (Butler) with Carmen de Lavallade
Kwamina musical comedy choreographed by Agnes de Mille with important cast of Black dancers

1962   Ailey Company at ADF
District Storyville (McKayle)
Dudley Williams in Martha Graham Company
A Midsummer Night's Dream (Balanchine) NYCB with Mitchell as Puck
Bamboche revue by Katherine Dunham and Company
Chubby Checker makes films featuring the twist
National Dance Theatre Company (NDTC) founded

(Jamaica)
Feast of Ashes (Ailey)

1963   Destine at ADF
McKayle at ADF choreographed by Katherine Dunham for New York
Aida Metropolitan Opera

1964   Gus Solomons in Young Choreographers Series at YMHA

1965   *Four Marys* (de Mille) with Cleo Quitman, Judith Jamison, Glory Van Scott, and Carmen de Lavallade
Percussion Suite (Rod Rodgers)
Echoes of Jazz TV film with McKayle, William Louther, and Mary Hinkson
Junkie (Pomare)

1966   First World Festival of Negro Art (Senegal)
Judith Jamison and George Faison join Ailey Company
Blues for the Jungle (Pomare)
Anthony and Cleopatra choreographed by Alvin Ailey for New York Metropolitan Opera

1967   *Las Desenamoradas* (Pomare)
New Dance Group organized by Molly Ahye (Trinidad)
Katherine Dunham begins work in East St. Louis

1968   Percival Borde teaches at ADF
Hair musical with integrated cast of singers, dancers
Narcissus Rising (Pomare)
Tangents (Rodgers)
Louis Johnson at Negro Ensemble Company
Acrobats of God (Graham) filmed version includes Hinkson, Clive Thompson and William Louther

1969   Beatty teaches at ADF
Ailey company at ADF
Masakela Langage (Ailey/Masakela)
Dance Theatre of Harlem (DTH) founded
Alvin Ailey American Dance Center founded

1970   Walter Nicks and Clay Taliaferro teach at ADF
The River (Ailey)
Streams (Ailey)
Black Cowboys (Rodgers)

1971   DTH appears with NYCB in *Concerto of Jazz Band and Orchestra*
Cry (Ailey)
Gazelle (Faison)
Kasamance book by Katherine Dunham published

1972   *Love Songs* (Ailey)
The Lark Ascending (Ailey)
Forces of Rhythm (Louis Johnson)
Sounds in Motion founded by Diane McIntyre
Break dancing becomes prominent

1973 First National Congress on Blacks in Dance (Indiana
University)
Dance Theatre of Harlem at ADF
Inner City Repertory Dance Company at ADF in
McKayle repertory
Carmen choreographed by Alvin Ailey for New
York Metropolitan Opera

1974 Charles Moore Company founded
Suite Otis (Faison/Otis Redding songs)
Bill F. Jones/Arnie Zane season at Joyce Theater
"Ailey Celebrates Ellington"

1975 *The Wiz* musical directed by Geoffrey Holder and
choreographed by George Faison
Night Creatures (Ailey/Ellington)

1976 Thelma Hill Performing Arts Center founded by Larry
Phillips
Bubbling Brown Sugar revue choreographed by Billy
Wilson
Chuck Davis African Dance Company at ADF
Walter Nicks Dance Theater at ADF
Three Black Kings (Ailey)
Blood Memories (McKayle)

1977 FESTAC – Festival of Black Arts (Nigeria)

1978 *From Before* (Fagan)
Ailey 20th Anniversary Gala. Dunham, McBurnie,
Primus honored
The Wiz film choreographed by Louis Johnson

1979 ADF features Alvin Ailey Company and Arthur Hall
Company. Hall and Walter Nicks on faculty

No Maps on My Taps film

1980 Thelma Hill Performing Arts Center, A Celebration of
Men in Dance including Randolph Sawyer, Al
Bledger, Tommy Gomez, Joe Nash, John Hines
Fame film

1981 *Chicken Soup* Blondell Cumming
Etude on Free (Dianne McIntyre)
Remembering Thelma film about Thelma Hill made
by Kathe Sandler

1982 Mel Tomlinson at NYCB in Balanchine's Persephone
Film: *The Spirit Moves* (Mura Dehn)

1983 Dance Black America Festival at the Brooklyn
Academy of Music (BAM)
Precipice (Alvin Ailey for the Paris Ballet)
Flashdance film

1984 DTH produces "creole" version of *Giselle*

1985 Honi Coles receives Dance Magazine Award
White Nights film

1986 *CON/TEXT* (Gus Solomons)

1988 The Philadelphia Dance Company (Phildanco) con-
venes the First Annual International Conference
on Black Dance Companies, Philadelphia, Pa.
ADF begins three-year project The Black Tradition in
American Modern Dance, Durham, N.C.

1989 The Caribbean Cultural Center, New York City,
presents A Search for Roots: The Life and Work of
Dr. Pearl Primus – An Exhibit.

Bibliography

(In general, newspaper and magazine sources are given in the text.)

Allen, Zita. *Alvin Ailey American Dance Theater.* 25th anniversary program. [1983]

Alvin Ailey American Dance Theater, The. Photography by Susan Cook. Commentary by Joseph J. Mazo. New York: William Morrow, 1978.

Alvin Ailey American Dance Theater, 1958–1978. 20th anniversary program.

Ames, Jerry and Jim Siegelman. *The Book of Tap.* New York: David McKay & Co., 1977.

Anderson, Jack. *The American Dance Festival.* Durham, N.C.: Duke University Press, 1987.

Ardoin, John. *The Stages of Menotti.* Garden City, N.Y.: Doubleday & Co., 1985.

Arvey, Verna. *Choreographic Music.* New York: E. P. Dutton & Co., 1941.

Ayhe, Molly. *Cradle of Caribbean Dance: Beryl McBurnie and the Little Carib Theater.* Port of Spain: Heritage Cultures, 1983.

Ayhe, Molly. *Golden Heritage: The Dance in Trinidad and Tobago.* Port of Spain: Heritage Cultures, 1978.

Baker, Joséphine and Bouillon, Jo, *Joséphine.* Paris: Editions Robert Laffont, 1976.

Ballet Africains de Keita Fodeba. Program. [1959]

Barnes, Sally. *Terpsichore in Sneakers: Post-Modern Dance.* Boston: Houghton-Mifflin, 1980.

Barber, Beverly Anne Hillsman. "Pearl Primus, In Search of Her Roots: 1943–1970." Ph.D. dissertation, Florida State University, 1984.

Baxter, Ivy. *The Arts of an Island.* Metuchen, N.J.: The Scarecrow Press, 1970.

Beaumont, Cyril W. *Michel Fokine and His Ballets.* New York: Dance Horizons, 1981 (reprint).

Bordman, Gerald. *American Musical Theatre: A Chronicle.* New York: Oxford University Press, 1978.

Buckle, Richard. *Katherine Dunham: Her Dancers, Singers, Musicians.* London: Ballet Publishers [1947]

Caribe. "Special Dance Issue." Vol. VII, nos. 1 & 2.

Cluzel, Magdeleine E. *Glimpses of the Theatre and Dance* (trans. Lily and Baird Hastings). New York: Kamin Publishers, 1953.

Croce, Arlene. *After Images.* New York: Vintage Books, 1979 (Knopf, 1977).

Dance: Black America. Programme. April 21–24, 1983. Brooklyn Academy of Music.

Dance Magazine, Editors. *The Gospel According to Dance.* Text by Giora Manor. New York: St. Martin's Press, 1980.

De Mille, Agnes. *Dance to the Piper.* Boston: Little Brown and Co., 1951.

Denby, Edwin. *Dance Writings,* ed. Robert Cornfield and William Mackey. New York: Alfred A. Knopf, 1986.

Duncan, Isadora. *My Life.* New York: Bow and Liveright, 1927.

Duncan, Isadora ed. Paul Magriel. New York: Henry Holt & Co., 1947.

Dunham, Katherine. *The Dances of Haiti.* Los Angeles: Center for Afro-American Studies, UCLA, 1983. (also published as "Las Danzas de 'Haiti" *Acta Anthropologica* (Mexico, 1947) and *Les Danses d'Haiti* (Paris: Fasquel, 1957).

Dunham, Katherine. "The Negro Dance," in *The Negro Caravan,* ed. Sterling A. Brown, Arthur V. Davis and Ulysses Lee. New York: Dryden Press, 1941, pp. 991–1000.

Emery, Lynn, *Black Dance in the United States From 1617 to 1970.* Palo Alto, Calif.: National Press Bureau, 1972.

Ewen, David. *Complete Book of the American Musical Theater.* New York: Henry Holt, 1959.

Fowler, Carolyn. *Black Arts and Black Aesthetics.* Atlanta, Ga.: First World Press, 1981.

Freedley, George. "The Black Crook and the White Fawn" in *Chronicles of the American Dance* ed. Paul Magriel. New York: Henry Holt & Co., 1978, pp. 65–79.

Gruen, John. *The Private World of Ballet.* New York: The Viking Press, 1975.

Harmon, Terry. *African Rhythm, American Dance: A Biography of Katherine Dunham.* New York: Alfred A. Knopf, 1974.

Haskins, Jim (James). *The Cotton Club.* New York: Random House, 1977.

Haskins, James. *Katherine Dunham.* New York: Coward, McCann and Geoghegan, 1982.

Hatch-Billops Collection. *Artists and Influences: 1981.* New York.

Hemenway, Robert E. *Zora Neale Hurston: A Literary Biography.* Urbana: University of Illinois Press, 1978.

Hirschhorn, Clive. *The Hollywood Musical.* New York: Crown Publishing, 1981.

Hodgson, Maria. *Quartet: Five American Dance Companies.* Photographs by Thomas Victor. New York: William Morrow and Company, 1976.

Horst, Louis, *Modern Dance Forms* ed. Carroll Russell. Princeton, N.J.: Dance Horizons, 1987 (reprint of c. 1961 ed.).

Humphrey, Doris. *The Art of Making Dances.* New York: Grove Press, 1959.

Hurok, S. *S. Hurok Presents: A Memoir of the Dance World.* New York: Hermitage House, 1953.

Isaacs, Edith V. R. *The Negro in the American Theatre.* College Park, Md.: McGrath Publishing Co., 1968 (reprint of c. 1947 ed.).

Kirby, Michael, ed. *Happenings.* New York: E. P. Dutton & Co., 1965.

Kirstein, Lincoln. *Thirty years: The New York City Ballet.* 2nd ed. New York: Alfred A. Knopf, 1978.

Koegler, Horst, ed. *The Concise Oxford Dictionary of Ballet.* Oxford: Oxford University Press, 1977.

Lauffe, Abe. *Broadway's Greatest Musicals.* New York: Funk and Wagnall, 1969.

Lloyd, Margaret. *The Borzoi Book of Modern Dance.* New York: Dance Horizons, 1974 (reprint of Knopf edition of 1944).

Locke, Alain, The Critical Temper of: . . . Essays on Art and Culture. Ed. Jeffrey C. Stewart. New York: Garland Publishing, 1983.

Locke, Alain. "The Negro and the American Stage." *Theater Arts Monthly* 10 (February 1926): pp. 112–20.

Long, Richard A. *Black Americana.* Secaucus, N.J.: Chartwell, 1985.

Long, Richard A. "Black Influences on Choreography of the American Musical Theatre Since 1930," in *Musical Theater in America,* ed. Glenn Loney. Westport: Greenwood Press, 1984.

Long, Richard A. "The Outer Reaches: The White Writer and Blacks in the Twenties," in *The Harlem Renaissance Re-Examined,* ed. Victor A. Kramer. New York: AMS Press, 1988.

McDonagh, Don. *The Rise and Fall and Rise of Modern Dance.* New York: New American Library, 1971 (reprint of c. 1970 ed.).

Macdougal, Allan Ross. *Isadora: A Revolutionary in Art and Love* New York: Thomas Nelson & Sons, 1960.

Martin, John. *The Dance.* New York: Tudor, 1946.

Martin, John. *John Martin's Book of the Dance.* New York: Tudor, 1963.

Martin, K. K. "America's First African Dance Theatre" *Caribe* 7 (nos. 1 & 2): pp. 6–10.

Mazo, Joseph H. *Prime Movers: Makers of Modern Dance in America.* Princeton, N.J.: Princeton Book Co., 1979.

Myers, Gerald, ed. *The Black Tradition in American Modern Dance.* Durham, N.C.: American Dance Festival, 1988.

Nettleford, Rex. *Dance Jamaica: Cultural Definition and Artistic Discovery.* Photographs by Maria La Yacona. New York: Grove Press, 1985.

Nettleford, Rex. *Roots and Rhythms: Jamaica's National Dance Theatre.* Photographs by Maria La Yacona. New York: Hill and Wang, 1969.

Nicholson, Josephine Monica. "Three Black Pioneers in American Modern Dance, 1931–1945." M.A. thesis, School of Educational and Human Development, New York University, 1984.

Palmer, Winthrop. *Theatrical Dancing in America.* 2nd ed., rev. New York: A. S. Barnes & Co., 1978.

Parker, David L. and Eleanor Siegel. *Guide to Dance in Film.* Detroit: Gale Research Co., 1978.

Primus, Pearl. "An Anthropological Study of Masks as Teaching Aids in the Enculturation of Mano Children." Ph.D. dissertation, New York University, 1978.

Rogosin, Elinor. *The Dance Makers: Conversations with American Choreographers.* New York: Walker, 1980.

Schlundt, Christena L. *Ruth St. Denis and Ted Shawn: A Chronology.* New York: The New York Public Library, 1962.

Schlundt, Christena L. *Ted Shawn and His Men Dancers: A Chronology.* New York: The New York Public Library, 1967.

Seldes, Gilbert. *The 7 Lively Arts.* New York: Sagamore Press, 1957 (reprint of c. 1924 ed.).

Shelton, Suzanne. *Divine Dancer: A Biography of Ruth St. Denis.* New York: Doubleday & Co., 1981.

Sherman, Jane. *The Drama of Denishawn Dance.* Middleton, Conn.: Wesleyan University Press, 1987.

Siegel, Marcia B. *Days on Earth: The Dance of Doris Humphrey.* New Haven: Yale University Press, 1987.

Simpson, Herbert M. "Gus Solomons: 'Make No Boxes to Put Me In.' " *Dance Magazine* (September 1980): pp. 78–83.

Stearns, Marshall and Jan Stearns. *Jazz Dance: The Story of American Vernacular Dance.* New York: Shirmer paperback, 1979; Macmillan, 1968.

Sun Over the West Indies. Program. Howard University, Friday, May 19 [1961]

Terry, Walter. *Ted Shawn: Father of American Dance.* New York: Dial Press, 1976.

Toll, Robert C. *Blacking Up: The Minstrel Show in Nineteenth Century America.* New York: Oxford University Press, 1974 (paperback, 1977).

Van Vechten, Carl, The Dance Writings of, ed. Paul Padgette. New York: Dance Horizons, 1974.

Vaughan, David. *Frederick Ashton and His Ballets.* New York: Alfred A. Knopf, 1977.

Williams-Yarborough, Lavinia. *Haitian Dance.* [Port-au-Prince, n.p., n.d.]

Winter, Marion Hannah. "Juba and American Minstrelsy" in *Chronicles of the American Dance,* ed. Paul Magriel, New York: Henry Holt, 1948, pp. 39–63.

Index

Photographic Acknowledgements

Pictures supplied throughout by the Joe Nash Black Dance Collection, New York Public Library (Schomburg Collection), including those on pages: 5, 77 (Gerda Petrich); 6, 7, 143 *below*, 144, 145 *above*, 146 *below*, 149 *below* (Jack Mitchell); 9, 10 (Rockefeller Folk Art Collection, Williamsburg, Virginia); 114–15, 117 *right*, 118 *below*, 120, 138 *below*, 154 *above*, 155 *right*, 156, 158 *above* (Martha Swope); 18, 172 *below* (Lois Greenfield); 56 (Gjon Mili); 59 (Boris Bokchy); 64 (Serge Lido), 68 *above*, 101, 102 (Carmen Schiavone); 67 *right*, 98, 124 *below left*, 159 *below*, 162 *below*, 172 *above* (Thelma Hill Performing Arts Center); 78, 92 *below* courtesy Pearl Primus; 83 *right* (Gene Schmidt); 84 courtesy Donald McKayle; 87 (George Lake); 88–9, 90 *below* courtesy Arthur Mitchell; 90 *above* (Peter Kaufman); 91 courtesy (Martin Dain) Geoffrey Holder; 92 *above* (Morgan & Marvin Smith); 95 (Marcus Bleckman); 97, 99 courtesy Katherine Dunham; 103 (John Von Lund); 104–5, 126 *below* (Metropolitan Opera Association); 106 (Louise Jefferson); 107, 108 courtesy Dinizulu; 109 courtesy Ella Moore; 110 (John Lindquist); 111 (Jay Anderson); 112 courtesy Arthur Hall; 116, 146 *above* courtesy Alvin Ailey; 117 *left* (Anthony Crickmay); 118 *above* courtesy John Jones; 122 (Peter Garrick), 123 courtesy Sylvester Campbell; 124 *above left* courtesy Ward Flemyng; 126 *above* courtesy Raven Wilkinson; 127 (Marty Sohl); 128 (Sandy Geis); 131 (Jay Anderson); 135 (Atsushi Iijima); 136 (Norman Maxon); 137 *above*, 150, 152 *below* (Johan Elbers); 137 *below* (Maria Aguilera), 138 *above* (Walter Owens); 139, 152 *above*, 153 *above left* (Kenn Duncan); 140, 142 courtesy Eleo Pomare; 141 *above* (Einer Berg); 145 *below* (Dominic); 147 *above*, 149 *above*, 153 *above right* (Jack Vartoogian); 147 *below* (Bill Hilton); 148 (George Kalinsky); 151 (Max Waldman); 155 *left* (Dance Theatre of Harlem Archives); 157 (Bill King, courtesy *Vanity Fair*); 158 *below* (Guido Pater Nesi); 159 *above left* (Max Yves Brandilly); 161 courtesy Jeraldyne Blunden; 162 *above* (Kevin Keister, Herald-Sun Papers); 163 (Deborah Boardman); 164 (New Dance Theater Collection); 165 (Van Williams); 167 (Audrian); 168, 169 (Jennifer Gerard); 170 (Joe Nash); 174 courtesy Rael Lamb; 175 (E. Joseph Jr.).

Additional photographs supplied by New York Public Library, Schomburg Collection: 14 *below*, 15, 26, 28 *below*, 33 *right* (Gjon Mili), 34 *below* (Murray Korman), 42 (Twentieth Century Fox), 71, 93, 96; The Armstead Johnson Foundation for Theater Research Exhibit – Black America on Stage: 17, 27; The Black Patti Research Project (Delilah Jackson): 33 *left*, 34 *above*; National Dance Theatre of Jamaica: 176, 177, 178–9 *left*, 34 *above*; National Dance Theatre of Jamaica; 176, 177, 178–9 (Maria La Yacona); 155 *below* courtesy of Walter Raines.

The publishers have endeavored to observe the legal requirements with regard to the rights of suppliers of photographic material.

LIBRARY - Islington Sixth Form Centre

LIBRARY - Islington Sixth Form Centre